TOWARD
AN INTERIOR SUN

Also by Max Reif

Books
    Journey from here to HERE (poetry, 2013)
    Every Day Music (poetry, 2008)
    Canticles for Meher (poetry, 1985)

Audiocassette
    Inside Jobs: Stories for Adults and Other Kids (1997)

TOWARD AN INTERIOR SUN

Awakening by a Master, and the
Difficult Journey Toward Discipleship

Stories

MAX REIF

the mindful word

Published by The Mindful Word
Copyright © 2016 by Max Reif
ISBN 978-1-988245-59-1 (paperback) | ISBN 978-1-988245-60-7 (ebook)
ISBN 978-1-988245-61-4 (audiobook)

All rights reserved. No part of this publication may be reproduced, stored in a retrieval system or transmitted in any form or by any means—electronic, mechanical, photocopy, recording or any other—except for brief quotations, without the prior permission of the publisher.

Cover design: Dew Media
Cover art: "City/Self Mandala" by Max Reif
Author photo: Eddie Brooks
Photo of Meher Baba taken circa 1925: G. M. Shah
All the pieces in this book originally appeared in The Mindful Word

Printed in the United States of America

The Mindful Word
1120 Finch Ave. W. Unit 701-928
Toronto, Ontario
M3J 3H7, Canada

Visit us at www.themindfulword.org

Library and Archives Canada Cataloguing in Publication

Reif, Max, author
    Toward an interior sun : awakening by a master, and the difficult journey toward discipleship / Max Reif.

Issued in print and electronic formats.
ISBN 978-1-988245-59-1 (paperback).--ISBN 978-1-988245-60-7 (ebook)

    1. Reif, Max. 2. Meher Baba, 1894-1969. 3. Spirituality.
I. Title.

BL624.R446 2016   C2016-905960-X
                            C2016-905961-8

To the Highest inherent in all

and the labor of love to unveil it.

Contents

Preface i
Foreword: A Spiritual Life iii
Introduction v
Acknowledgments ix
STORIES 1
    Florida 3
    Prelude To A Wagnerian Springtime 15
    The Incident 23
    Summer of '68 37
    Coming Into It 63
    Fare To Malcolm Bliss 75
    The Key Turned 85
    Falling Off The Map 111
    Alternating Current 141
    The Life You Save May Be Your Own 157
    Adieu, Rivendell 173
APPENDIX: Two Essays 211
    My 45-Year Romance With Meher Baba 213
    Happy Re-Birthday To Me! 223

PREFACE

We're all storytellers by birth. But the disconcerting thing is that most of the stories we tell go to waste. They stay inside our minds, creating an endless stream of mental pictures that unconsciously end up guiding our actions. The great thing about writing is its ability to unleash these mental pictures onto the page for all (or just yourself) to read. Certain writers have a way of authentically expressing in words the images floating around in their heads with such vividness that it inspires readers to draw inwards and reflect. Max Reif is one of those writers.

I've had the pleasure of editing Max's submissions to The Mindful Word over the past couple of years. Whether it's a tale of fiction or real-life drama, his stories hook my attention from the beginning and keep me engaged until the end. What characterizes his writing most for me is his capacity to bring a story to life while giving us a window into ourselves.

The title of one of the stories in this collection, "My 45-Year Romance with Meher Baba," points to the source of Max's inspiration. Meher Baba was a spiritual guide for so many. He was a loving, wise soul who knew the needs of the people and selflessly tended to those needs. Meher Baba is the thread that Max weaves throughout his writings in one way or another. Baba inspired Max to dig deep into his mind and Max has generously offered readers the results of Baba's gift: a gift that the late Baba would no doubt be happy to see being passed on to future generations.

Toward an Interior Sun invites readers to do more than just read, but to ponder. It invites readers to sit back and be entertained, but to also engage themselves with curiosity. But most of all, the authentic nature of the stories in this book inspire readers to develop a true thirst for the truth.

Kiva Bottero
Editor, The Mindful Word
September, 2014

Foreword: A Spiritual Life

Max Reif in this book of stories and essays, largely autobiographical, has woven his troubled journey from boyhood to a place of love, devotion and joy. His well-worded stories take the reader — nay, the seeker — to attainable spiritual insights.

In his life-long devotion to Avatar Meher Baba, Max combines poetic expression with exploration of the known — and oftentimes, the unknown. He confesses, "in the late '60s, many of us were too young or immature to know the stakes." He experimented with drugs, as did many young people in the sixties, to get a "glimpse" of God through psychedelic drugs. A meeting with an old friend brought Max to the threshold of one who called himself the Ancient One — Meher Baba.

Max was being prepared for a spiritual life. The finest exchange in the book is between this friend and Max:

"Did Meher Baba really say he was *God*?" I asked.

"He says everyone and every*thing* is God, but there are very few who are fully *conscious* of that Divinity and who therefore are really able to guide others."

It was as T. S. Eliot called it "the timeless moment" for Max. He realized that Meher Baba was not only the Way and the Goal; he was the *only* Way and the Goal on his spiritual journey. As Max became transformed from a "dangerous pharmacological" past, he was convinced that following Meher Baba and holding onto his hand was the fast track to conscious divinity that his college friend had referred to.

Toward an Interior Sun is a door that opens in degrees to those who are willing to "walk on fire" as did Max. He is honest in his narration of experiences that span a lifetime. Sometimes life is like a river that flows quietly along the riverbed. Suddenly, the calm waters become a raging rapid, a maelstrom of waves that can both engulf and overwhelm. The stories and essays in this book reflect a life lived beyond just words.

Sometime back Max sent an essay to me that reflected his innermost thoughts and feelings. I quote the last paragraph, *"In the end, I am totally alone with Meher Baba, and sooner or later He will Show me where I really am. And sooner or later, whether in one or in a million lives, I will be One with Him. Until then, I'm in the Crucible of learning what 'my best' really is. And of learning what Faith in Him is, when His Grace works other than to Light my way and let me feel — if not see — His Face."*

It is in this Crucible of Learning that aspirants go through their spiritual journey—a swim from this shore to that shore. A walk from the transitory, ephemeral "seen" to the loving, compassionate "unseen" world that Meher Baba promises we will inherit.

Max Reif knows. Max Reif understands. Max Reif is on his way.

Naosherwan Anzar
Beloved Archives
20 September 2015

INTRODUCTION

If I had taken my younger self aside, as if we were in some "Back to the Future" movie, and told him what he would be going through in coming decades, I don't think he would have believed me! The life that has unfolded has astounded me in its glorious heights as well as, sometimes, its dismal depths. Most remarkable of all, perhaps, has been learning that rebirth, redemption, and a fresh new page are *always* possible, even after the darkest night. It is these insights that have set my spirit and hand in motion to write the pieces collected in this book.

The stories are drawn from my life, and with few exceptions are true records of events. I have changed names of people and places. I subscribe to the current meme that memory is a narrative and not necessarily an absolutely accurate record. At the same time, I believe that the essence, the heart of memory, carries existential truth for that soul.

Every story *or* memoir is about life and its vast possibilities. The merit of either genre lies in its success in providing readers with vicarious *experiences* that are universal, true, and significant.

I believe that all of us are on Earth at a most fortuitous time. Every seven hundred to fourteen hundred years, as I understand it, the Avatar, also known as the Christ, Buddha, or Rasool—the World Messenger— returns to Earth to remind us all why we are here, and to take us a little bit farther toward our true potential. The last six stories in the main body of this book dramatize events taking place after my life's watershed experience, the *meeting* of Meher Baba, whom thousands believe to be that Messenger, in January, 1971. This was a spiritual meeting rather than a physical one, as Baba had passed away physically "to live forever in the hearts of His lovers" in 1969. But having read the accounts of many people who met Meher Baba when he was in the body, I don't find a qualitative difference. And indeed, the Master himself likened his physical death to merely taking off a coat.

There is no way to fully convey in words the experience of meeting God, unless God Himself helps both the person recounting the experience and the person listening or reading. My essay in this book's Appendix, "My Forty-Five Year Romance with Meher Baba" goes as far as I can go in that direction.

If it were not for Baba, and for one of his helpers, Richard Alpert, aka Ram Dass, I believe my life, or at least its "story," would have ended in my twenties. Almost every one of the tales in *Toward an Interior Sun* is about rebirth, redemption, and possibility.

Mine has been a difficult journey, and yet the Light far outshines the difficulty, and the difficulty leaves me grateful beyond words for the Light. In one of my favorite quotes, Meher Baba describes spiritual wayfaring as "laboriously traversing the path with slow and bleeding steps" (*Beams from Meher Baba*, pp. 50-51).

Here is brief synopsis of the eleven stories in the book:

FLORIDA—James Joyce gave us the concept of "epiphanies" in writing. This tale of a boy being admitted briefly to his own imagination's idea of an earthly paradise prefigured later "mystical" experiences.

PRELUDE TO A WAGNERIAN SPRING—A tale of first love, and my initial experience of the utterly impossible actually coming to pass, mostly due to forces beyond my ego's control.

THE INCIDENT—The event narrated in this story took place in 1967 on the campus of Northwestern University. The winds of change were in the air. The insular self-image with which I had left the home nest in the fall received a death blow.

SUMMER OF '68—Rebirth after the "little death" of lost love. Each time such a thing occurs, we feel broken beyond repair. And if we are fortunate, we learn to our amazement that, as Henry Miller once wrote, "The human heart cannot be broken," at least not in the depths from which new life springs.

COMING INTO IT—This story takes place at "Erewhon College" (New College) in Sarasota, Florida. It describes the seduction of psychedelics, in this case to blast through deeply-buried problems. Each time the dice roll, the brass ring appears to be in reach; but in the end, it's a slippery slope.

FARE TO MALCOLM BLISS—Fast forward a few years. "Martin" is now a "Baba-Lover," (the initial experience with Meher Baba is briefly narrated in this story). He drives a taxi through the St. Louis night. Baba's smiling face on a dashboard card counsels passengers, DON'T WORRY—BE HAPPY. On a rainy night, a remarkable and challenging adventure ensues.

THE KEY TURNED—Martin has revelations and inspired periods that are clearly Divine Grace. But he also feels the need for human love—and as Baba said, "Human love leads to innumerable complications and tangles...." (*The Path of Love*, "Love and God-Love," pp. 67-71) The karma of human *and* divine love lead him to his first pilgrimage to Baba's Samadhi (Tomb-Shrine) near Ahmednagar, India.

FALLING OFF THE MAP—Human love combined with human frailty lead to incarceration for kicking a policeman in the shin, and set in motion a cycle of events that appear impossible to recover from.

GAIL—In the early 1980's, Martin again loses his way. This time he experiences ECT, better known as shock treatments. Afterward, he despairs because although the treatments stopped his mind's racing, they closed off his heart. His recovery from that condition comes in a most surprising way!

THE LIFE YOU SAVE MAY BE YOUR OWN—Art becomes the key to delivery from yet another impossible situation!

ADIEU, RIVENDELL—Martin seems to realize his dream to be able to live the rest of his life near the Meher Spiritual Center, a retreat facility and wildlife refuge in Myrtle Beach, South Carolina. This, too, does not work out as he had hoped. "Leaving God to find God," he discovers yet again that the streams of Love are indeed always flowing, and persistent effort to re-connect with them pays off.

Some readers may wish to begin with this book's two Appendix pieces. The first one tells the story of my "coming to Baba." The second tells the tale of a crisis five years later, when "stuff from my childhood" came to the surface and I was being driven toward suicide. Via the greatest serendipity, I ended up sitting with Ram Dass in his room in the Downtowner Motel in Oklahoma City, the morning after one of his talks, "told him everything I couldn't tell anybody," and left the room free of the shame that was killing my life, and has never returned.

Max Reif
Walnut Creek, California
July 31, 2016

Acknowledgments

Thanks to many, many people who have helped me to arrive at a fairly happy age 68, which might have surprised my 21 year-old self! Special appreciation to my wife Barbara for 17 years of loving companionship, and now for formatting and helping to edit this book; and to my parents, Irwin and Corinne Reif, for "hanging in" with me during some difficult years.

To Avatar Meher Baba and people connected with Him all over the world.

Special mention to several mentors: Ram Dass; Lyn Ott; Jal S. Irani; and Edward and Irwin Luck. Also, Kitty Davy and Jane Haynes at Meher Center in Myrtle Beach, South Carolina.

To Mr. Robert Clipner and Mr. James Hake, teachers whose encouragement got me thinking of myself as a writer; Mr. Emory Basford at Andover Academy and Miss Rothschild at U. City High, who inculcated an idea of "the good life" that I still resonate with; Francis Brabazon, Meher Baba's poet, whose work showed me that words can still have meaning; my college professor Michael Atkinson, always quietly encouraging; the folks from The Mindful Word: Jane Olivier, who started the ball rolling by asking to print some of my poems; Kiva Bottero and Erica Roberts; and Omar Willey of the *Seattle Star*, himself an inspired artist.

Finally: how to say this? All the characters in this Story we're living —friends, girlfriends—even the guys they left me for (ouch)! All leading me toward the One, as I gradually learn how to take the hint.

"It's not how many times you fall down; it's how many times you get back up."

–Anon.

"I'd like to tell my story, said one of them so bold.
I'd like to tell my story, because you know
I feel I'm turning into gold."

–Leonard Cohen, "A Bunch of Lonesome Heroes"

"When longing is most intense separation is complete, and the purpose of separation, which was that Love might experience itself as Lover and Beloved, is fulfilled; and union follows. And when union is attained, the Lover knows that he himself was all along the Beloved whom he loved and desired union with; and that all the impossible situations that he overcame were obstacles which he himself had placed in the path to himself."

–Meher Baba, *The Everything and the Nothing*

STORIES

Florida

1.

I've tried to tell the story of my family's motor trip to Florida, which I believe was in 1959, when I was eleven, many times before. One time I must have done fairly well, because *Mothering*, a pretty big magazine at the time, wrote me that they were very close to publishing it. At the last minute, they chose to use something else instead.

Writing down that version had all the magic of conjuring with a wand. It embodied the miracle of writing, the capacity of strange little black lines to bring forth a vision completely intact from within one person, and put it inside another person. Everyone who read the piece was able to experience the thrill of our three-day adventure through the kudzu-choked pine forests of the South, in the days before interstates, and then of the drive all the long, green way down the Florida peninsula.

Subsequent efforts to tell the story, after that first manuscript got lost during one of my many moves in the '80s and '90s, were duds. But the trip, my first impression of the world outside the womb of our hometown and its environs, still lives a mythic life in me. It is forever cut into my psyche in very bright, bold relief, beginning with my getting the earth-shaking news that it was going to happen.

2.

Dad informed us one day that a family meeting—a family meeting—us?—would take place in the dining room later that afternoon. There, he dropped the news that he and Grandpa were closing the furniture store and taking us, in our rocket-finned Dodge Coronet, to Miami Beach with some of the proceeds. I staggered out into the front yard, dazed.

Some of my friends' families, and my own grandparents, journeyed yearly to the Jewish Mecca in the South. Even our Christian neighbors, the Mortlands, had been to nearby Fort Lauderdale. However, I'd completely accepted that such boons were forever out of reach for our family. Now, suddenly, fortune had smiled upon me. Shafts of late-afternoon sunlight appropriately slanted down through the maples, onto the grass, like in a scene from a religious movie.

The two-week countdown to our leaving was, of course, agonizing. But we finally pulled away from all of our psyches' habitual moorings, except for one another and the intrepid car, in the still-dark of an early August morning.

3.

Everyone was much, much happier on the trip very soon after leaving, except possibly Mother, who wasn't much of an adventurer. I guess it was brave of her just to come along.

Dad's improvement began almost as soon as we left the curb. One of the many things I loved about Dad was that he always wanted to set out before the sun rose. I imagine all great adventures begin then, for where such things are concerned, who can wait? We even started before dawn on our Sunday fishing expeditions to Creve Coeur Lake, a few miles away.

Dad was taking a risk by embarking on this family trip at a time of personal economic uncertainty. Yes, he had a few bucks from the store sale, and he would have job prospects upon our return, but he was operating on blind trust that one of them would work out. They were all shoe-leather sales jobs, carpet or linoleum or furniture, and lately, his talk with Mom when he'd come home at night had sounded pretty stuffy to my brother and me. It was all "Garber said this," and "Courtney said that." The names were apparently those of prospective new bosses, but never having met the men, Fred and I couldn't even picture the faces that went with them.

Dad started off the trip by pouring out a residue of such blather across the front seat into Mom's ear, but as soon as we were out of the force field of St. Louis and our daily lives, it all dropped away. It was like some cleansing agent had gone through Dad's mind and taken away all the boring stuff! He came alive as Dad again. He even became Daddy, the one who'd introduced me not too many years before to the zoo, the circus, the Cardinals, Martin and Lewis movies, fishing, and Rockwood Reservation with its trails and cave, from which we'd plundered many a toad and garter snake, stuffing them into pillowcases and unloading them in the ancient bathtub in our basement. He started saying things like, "Hey, we just passed Red Bud, Illinois, and look—the sun's like a red bud!"

4.

We'd set off on deserted streets and crossed the Mississippi River half an hour later, as the very first rays of sun were pushing up. Then we drove south in Illinois along the Great River Road. I loved that name, as well as the big green logo of a ship's wheel that appeared on every highway marker.

Our previous forays into the green fields on the East Side, beyond the sorrowful ruin that was East St. Louis, had been to Stoplight All-You-Can-Eat Fried Chicken, and once or twice to the horse races at Cahokia and Fairmont. Before long we'd passed those turn-offs, and every sight became a new vision swimming in through my eyes.

5.

The real plot of this story doesn't begin until we near Miami Beach, so how can I best convey the adventure? I hope it isn't a cliché to say that the pioneers didn't only live in the 18th and 19th centuries—every person setting out beyond the boundaries of his or her life is a pioneer.

Yes, people had previously been where we drove, to build the state roads we took through the forests of Mississippi—probably the Works Progress Administration, back in the Great Depression, which had taken place a mere 20 years before. Someone had built the infrastructure, and someone else had built the new Holiday Inn motels that to us were bright, clean wilderness outposts. And yes, people lived in all these places we passed. It wasn't an adventure to them to be there. But of course, it would have been for them to drive out of *their* lives to where *we* lived.

Dad had traveled extensively, but that had been in another life. He'd told us stories about how he and his friend Higgins had thumbed around America and Mexico. Plus, during the Second World War, Dad had put together shows for troop morale and had traveled by train with his performers all over America, including the Deep South, where we were heading.

For me, this world was as unknown as the uncharted ocean had been to Columbus. I acted as navigator, holding our AAA TripTik, its route thickly outlined in sky-blue marker, on my lap and advising Dad. I ached for us to take the scenic route, which time did not allow, that swept down to the Gulf of Mexico through Mobile and Tampa, instead of inland through central Florida. Though my Florida dream was coming true, just around the corner were *more* dreams that remained elusive. This was, however, only about as pesky as a mosquito bite.

6.

That first day, we made it to Tupelo, Mississippi. To me, both place names sounded nearly as exotic as Morocco or Timbuktu. My dim awareness at that age scarcely comprehended the significance of, or history behind the Bill Crow laws that were still in effect all around us. On the narrow forest highways we traveled along, "White" and "Colored" signs were not even that common.

The second morning, we came to a rickety grey wood shack of a gas station in a tiny clearing by the side of the road, with only dusty ground surrounding the gas pump. We'd been going quite a while, and needed a bathroom. Mom had a Coke bottle in back for Fred and me to pee in, though that was always a risky, nearly acrobatic affair with the car moving, but sometimes we had to stop for "the other."

The whole site—station, tires and car parts strewn around, mangy sleeping dog, rusted trash barrels, absolute mess of a tiny office, greasy little garage—was utterly foreign to a Jewish family from a Midwestern suburb. Pulling up at the pump, Dad got out and went to scout out the bathrooms. A little later, he returned with a sour look on his face. I never got to see how bad it was. Dad got back in the car and turned on the ignition, just as a man who looked like Junior from *Hee Haw* emerged from the office, crossed in front of our car, and drawled, "Kin ah help y'all?"

Nonplussed and not wanting to offend, Dad began pulling away, at a loss for words. As an afterthought, he turned his head and shouted loudly to the man, "We'll come back later!" He was only trying to be polite, but the whole car erupted in laughter at his expense.

7.

We finally made it to a better place, or at least one that looked better, an actual restaurant some miles past the station. Overjoyed to finally be able to relieve ourselves, we then realized how hungry we were! The morning before in Cairo, Illinois, in full view of the confluence of the Mississippi and Ohio rivers, I'd had my first encounter with grits. Adding two pats of butter, I loved them! Fortunately, they came with our eggs here in Mississippi, too. As I dug into my delicious breakfast, safe at this table in the wagon-circle of our family, so to speak, I heard a little scream nearby. I looked up to see Mother looking ghost-white.

"What happened, dear?" asked Dad.

In reply, Mom picked up her nearly intact plate of eggs, grits and toast. She raised it up and began tipping it toward us, stopping just short of where the food would begin falling onto the table. Dad, Fred and I craned our heads forward and suddenly I saw what had made her scream. In the middle of Mother's grits was a hair! It was much too short to have come from her head. A moment later, the four of us were tromping back to the car in protest. I was just thankful that I was a fast eater!

8.

The next memorable thing was crossing into Alabama. It was not like a country character said in a story I read once, "State boundary? If you cain't see it, how come they put it on the map?" No, my "collection" of states was expanding so widely that I could scarcely contain my excitement!

Alabama was not *quite* as exciting as Mississippi, our first Deep South state, had been, until we got to Dothan, a very small town not too far from the Florida border. There, on a nondescript residential street that the highway narrowed to, were the first palm trees I'd ever seen actually growing out of the ground! Several tiny palmettos graced the front yard of a modest one-story house, so unobtrusive you could almost miss them. I must have lived my most recent lifetime in a tropical country, because as long as I can remember, I've been nuts about anything tropical. I drove my mother bananas (pardon the semi-pun), making her search St. Louis in the car with me for coconuts, mangoes and papayas, long before every supermarket carried them, until we finally found some at Straubs, the local hoity-toity store.

9.

Not long after Dothan, we crossed into Florida. Florida, Dad reminded me, is a *long* state. Mind-bogglingly, we were still 500 miles from Miami! We crossed the Suwanee River, which I'm not sure I had realized was a real place, and then swung south. Florida, it turned out, had "horse country" as well as its hundreds of square miles of citrus groves. We saw the latter from the top of Citrus Tower, a kind of little skyscraper in the middle of nowhere, exclusively for tourists.

On our last night on the road, we stopped at the Holiday Inn in Ocala. Here, I had a magical experience. Walking out to a traffic circle across from the hotel, I found a *grandfather* palm tree, no little houseplant-sized thing but a great, drooping green fountain of a date palm; an old, old tree with dozens, maybe hundreds of fronds. It had lovely little red, orange, and golden berry-fruits. Hundreds of birds roosted, fed on the fruit, and screeched in its branches, creating a fantastic, twittering din there just as day was yielding to dusk. So many things were happening! I felt as if I'd somehow stumbled into the center of the Great Mandala.

10.

Continuing south, we passed through part of the Everglades. I don't remember much water, though, only a lot of building and logging activity. At a tiny village called Clewiston, we had lunch at a big tourist trap called the Old South Bar-B-Que Ranch. It was impossible not to stop, as we'd been reading the restaurant's billboard ads for hundreds of miles. It was one of those places where you can stick your head in a hole behind a cowboy façade, and a family member can take your picture. My brother and I were young enough to get a charge out of it.

An hour or two later, we were driving through the streets of Miami's Little Havana. Most of the store signs and such were in Spanish. We drove a long way down some commercial boulevard with Jai-alai billboards and people I assumed were Cuban immigrants walking on the crowded sidewalks. Needless to say, I found this exciting. This street led to the causeway to Miami Beach—where, dear reader, our real plot commences.

11.

Our parents' marriage always had a fault line running through it. It was a "class" marriage, at least in Mother's mind, and sometimes that caused blowouts. "The Big One" never came, but there were some *pretty* big ones, as big as a child could imagine. One of these was the one of which rumblings began as we neared Miami Beach.

I'll delay the actual story a moment to give a bit more background and maybe create a bit of suspense, which all the Agatha Christie and Rex Stout books I've read lately have helped me value.

Mother and Dad shouldn't really have had any class rivalry, *except* that Dad was a second-generation American and Mother a third. Their ancestors had come from Russia and Lithuania, respectively, which I don't think made a difference, due to the German Jews, which neither of them were, supposedly making up the upper crust.

My Dad's father was a cabinetmaker. In America, he worked in a furniture factory and later owned, serially, several furniture stores and a moving business. Back in Europe, so the story goes, as an apprentice furniture-maker he'd had to go into the forest, fell a tree, and create furniture from all of its wood, remaining there alone until he'd finished. Sounds lovely, doesn't it?

Politically, back in the '30s, Grandpa had run as a Socialist for Treasurer of the city of St. Louis. When he retired after the furniture store closed, he devoted all his time to the garden he cultivated on the big corner lot where he and Grandma had their home. The sight of him in his sleeveless undershirt, patiently watering his flower beds, was an inspiration of my childhood. He also began to read his Bible seriously, and became an observant Conservative Jew. He died at 75 in 1968.

Mother's father, after whom I'm named, died just before I was born. Everyone I've met who knew him has said he was a kind man. He also looks that way in the pictures I've seen. He had a successful auto dealership in New York City until his willful wife, my grandmother whom I called "Maw," made him close it and move back to her home town of Lancaster, PA. Her father had owned a very prosperous scrap yard there, and her brother James somehow appropriated the whole thing for himself when the father died. The rest of the family sort of lived in the ruins of their former glory, like latter-day Scarlett O'Haras.

Drawing on this former glory, I suppose, Mother seemed to feel she came from patrician stock. She'd once dated a very wealthy New Yorker whose very name, Morganstern, sounds rich! But she broke up with him because she liked my father's personality, or at least that's what she always said. My father did have an infectious personality. He loved to tell jokes, and when he was young, he was also quite handsome.

Who knows, he might've even become wealthy himself, had he been able to pursue his chosen field, film. He'd loved movies from childhood on. From the '30s until the Second World War began and he enlisted in the army, he'd divided his time between Los Angeles and St. Louis. Out West, he studied acting at the Pasadena Playhouse and appeared as an extra in a number of films. He read gas meters as a day job.

He enlisted in the Army after Pearl Harbor, and rose to the rank of Major in the Signal Corps, where he worked, as I mentioned earlier, producing shows for troop morale. After the war was over and there were no more shows, he was put in charge of a big army film library in Long Island City, N.Y.

Mother happened to work there. One day, a mutual friend put her in touch with "that handsome officer" because she, a civilian, wanted to buy something at the Post Exchange (PX), where only army personnel were eligible for the sizable discount.

Dad's passion for film was so intense that he wanted to go back to California and go to film school on the GI Bill. He was very excited about this. Before their marriage, he had asked Mother if she'd accompany him, and she'd said yes. When push came to shove, though, she began to feel that to do so would be to abandon her mother on the

East Coast. California was too far away! Even St. Louis, where they finally settled because Dad couldn't find a job in New York after leaving the army and Grandpa had offered him a partnership in his furniture store, was like the Wild West to her.

Dad dropped all this information on me one morning as the two of us were breakfasting at Denny's when I was around 50. When Mom changed her mind, he said, I was already on the way. Had she not been pregnant, he said that he would have left. But his sense of responsibility toward a child, born or not, caused him to stay.

I occasionally imagine myself in his place, after what he certainly felt was a betrayal. When I do, my blood boils with resentment! That, coupled with the hated sales jobs he had to take for years, and the increasing complexity of fathering as we children got older, made his sometime shortness of temper understandable.

His resentment toward Mother seemed to dissipate as their 54-year marriage proceeded, until she told me proudly one day a few years before he died, "Dad told me yesterday that the thing he likes best in life is when he and I spend the afternoon shopping together at the mall."

12.

However, a certain turmoil *was* rumbling underground as we drove south in 1959. As we approached the fabled causeway that would take us to our destination, it boiled over!

Two people with two different visions are sure to run into trouble. Dad's idea was to ensconce ourselves at the Raleigh Hotel in South Miami Beach—the seedy, rather than trendy end of town in those days, where his own parents stayed for their yearly winter sojourns.

Mother, on the other hand, had presentiments of luxury. The Fontainebleau Hotel, that massive, curving vision of green glass, sang to her. She was like a showgirl who'd suddenly been called for her one big chance! She was Cinderella with one slipper. The other was made of curved green glass that fit perfectly!

13.

Having paid the toll at the booth for the causeway to Miami Beach, we'd arrived at showtime. Someone's vision was going to prevail, while someone else's would be trampled in the dust.

What began as a discussion rapidly became a shouting match, with insults thrown like horseshoes: "You want to stay where your parents stay—the same way you want me to wear my hair like your mother's! You never grew up!" To which my father replied, "We're not millionaires! Come down to Earth!"

Tempers flared to red-hot, then to white. My brother and I cringed, as we did during our parents' heated moments at home. I heard a sound and then saw that Mother had opened her car door and gotten out. She was opening the back door on my brother's side. "Come on, Fred!" she commanded. "We'll go to *our* hotel!" Fred followed obediently—as if you had much choice, with an angry parent. I sat where I was, feeling no more allegiance to one parent than another, but terrified to see our family break up before our eyes.

The temperature was in the '90s as Mom and Fred marched along the shoulder of the causeway, about to walk across Biscayne Bay. Dad put the car in gear and slowly drove alongside them, pleading, "*Please* come back. We'll go there for dinner; for God's sake! I promise!" Mother didn't even look his way. The road was devoid of traffic, allowing us to make the entire fantastic Miami Beach skyline the backdrop for our melodrama.

I can't remember exactly what it was that got them back in the car. Maybe he just wore her out. Something kept my parents together, just as something keeps my current wife and me, as contrasted with my earlier marital unions, together.

Half an hour later, we were checking in to the Raleigh, and that was fine with me! There was an open-air tropical juice bar a storefront away, where you could get all the papaya, coconut, or even papaya-coconut, that you wanted! Coconut palms waved in the air like hula dancers, and after a day or so, like old friends.

What was not to like? Despite a bit of trouble at the gate, I *had* arrived in paradise.

Prelude To A Wagnerian Springtime

1.
For a long time I didn't know her name, the pretty girl who'd come to our school in the fall of '61. I'd never heard her talk, either, and I imagined that she came from France. She wore her hair in shiny, brown curls. My favorite outfit of hers was a knee-length, form-fitting blue skirt combined with a pink blouse that accentuated her curves nicely.

A couple months after school started, my friend Ralph Frey took her to a party at our social club, the *Achim*—the Hebrew word for "Brothers," since the club met at the Jewish Community Center—was having, and we double-dated. That was how I learned her name was Leah, and that she came from Baltimore, not France.

Since we weren't yet 16, our fathers drove us to these parties that the club kept having because most of my friends were roaring with hormones and socially quite advanced for ninth graders. Many of these boys lived in the Delmar Loop tenements. Some had immigrant parents who gave them a lot of freedom. That was my mother's theory, anyway.

I was kind of an anomaly. It had taken a lot of what's commonly known as social climbing for me to get into this club. Once I *was* in, the boys, many of whom were the school's leaders and best athletes, had elected me president two years in a row. My impression was that they considered me some sort of *scholar*, and admired me for that.

My precociousness lagged way behind when it came to girls, though. Once a little time had elapsed since our last party, I'd start to dread our meetings. I knew someone would bring up having another one, and everyone would vote for it. But that meant I'd have to get a date, a thought which filled me with terror unmixed with any presentiment of joy.

My dating history had begun in seventh grade when a girl in my class had phoned me and asked if I knew the math assignment. Once I'd told her, she said, "Oh, and by the way, will you come to the sock hop with me?"

Talking to her that brief minute, I'd felt enormous discomfort. The sock hop, and the few dances and club parties I'd attended since, had all been emotional disasters for me. I'd kept up appearances by going, however, and so there were no untoward consequences—a week or two of nervous anticipation, ramped up during the event itself and followed by great relief after each one ended.

I worried about myself. My socially precocious friends had been talking about their sexual and romantic adventures since I'd first met them in seventh grade. One of them had described how allowing his dog to lick him had accidentally brought on his first ejaculation. Once they'd laughed about a "circle jerk," in which they'd taken turns masturbating into a coke bottle. I had no idea whether they were being truthful or making it up, possibly for the benefit of gullible, inexperienced me.

They talked about their exploits on Saturday nights "over at some girl's house" or in the balconies of the Varsity or Tivoli movie theatres in the Loop. I was almost 15 and I'd never kissed a girl or had an orgasm while awake. I wasn't even completely certain that the one or two "wet dreams" I thought I'd had hadn't really been bed-wetting episodes.

To tell the truth, I wasn't sure if what *anyone* said about sex was true. Maybe this whole idea of white stuff coming out of men's penises was just something people made up—a conspiracy, a prank they were playing on me. Once I'd had a dream that Randy Bornstein, the tallest, most physically mature boy and best athlete in our club, reached into my penis and pulled out some sperm, like a tribal elder priming my pump.

Prelude To A Wagnerian Springtime

Our party passed like the others had. To tell you the truth, I don't even remember who I brought. Ralph's dad picked us up. As he drove, he kept making left turns, joking that his steering wheel was stuck and couldn't turn right.

In the living room of the Finley's house, where the party was, I saw the usual couples, soon to be making out on the sofas. Dick Hart, whose basketball moves were quick as lightning, stood talking with his girlfriend, Gilda. Randy Bornstein had an arm around Sheila Mink. Seeing them together always lit a little flame of embarrassment in me. At a JCCA event, I *had* once gotten the nerve to ask Sheila to dance, not knowing that she and Randy had already fallen in love.

Nate Brandon and Cherie Shuman; Greg Moriarty and Lanie Bernstein; and Mark Vinsky and Lisa Ferdman, three inseparable couples, stood in a circle eating, drinking and laughing.

Most of the *Achim* picked their dates and girlfriends from the same group of girls. Ralph's bringing Leah was bold, but Ralph never lacked confidence where girls were concerned.

There seemed to be a distinct order of status among the pool of girls we chose from, as distinct as in any Polynesian or African tribe. I was hard put to understand this social ranking, but I accepted it, subtly deferring to the more popular girls and looking down slightly on the ones who, for some reason, were at the periphery of acceptability.

There were two sisters, for example, both of them in our grade. Whether they were non-identical twins, I still don't know. One of them was very popular. Her name was Susan. I would be doomed to forever label her in my thoughts as "Runaround Sue," after seeing her jitterbugging to that currently popular song with Sam Sanders at our party that night.

She and Sam were sort of like boyfriend and girlfriend for a while, though they never really went steady. I remember him walking her to the refreshment table after the song, *steering* her with an arm behind her waist. It reminded me a little of the way you might guide a mule. I wondered if *that* was how a boy was supposed to lead a girl.

Sam was a passionate boy, fast on a playing field, with flaming curls of brilliant orange hair. For the past year, he'd been so possessed by the rising sap of testosterone that half of what came out of his mouth, it seemed, was crudely sexual.

Somehow Susan, an intelligent and cultured young woman, gravitated to him. Susan's sister Mindy, on the other hand, didn't seem to be quite as popular. She often seemed slightly nervous. Probably just hadn't quite "come into herself" yet. I always tried to play it safe and ask "acceptable" girls to our parties, and when I once told someone I was thinking of asking Mindy, the approval ratings seemed weak.

After the party where Ralph and Leah doubled with my unmemorable date and me, I didn't talk to Leah for quite awhile. I'd see her in the halls occasionally. Now that we'd been introduced, I'd nod to her and she'd nod or wave back.

A couple months later, though, in January, I happened to find her outside of one of my classes as I exited, heading in the same direction I was. We walked together. Our conversation was easy and light. Thereafter, we became frequent hallway companions during the four or five minutes between classes.

Looking back, I have my doubts whether even that first meeting was a coincidence. Though I've already established that I wasn't Casanova, I was making a name for myself in some areas of school life. I'd become co-editor of the school newspaper and had won an area-wide journalism competition.

I'd also surprised everyone, including myself, by winding up as a starting guard and linebacker on the football team, rising from third string in the first few weeks of practice after going out for a sport I'd scarcely ever played. I even got the male lead in Victor Herbert's musical, "The Red Mill," though I burned in fires of ironic embarrassment every time I had to sing my solo, a song called "Every Day is Ladies' Day with Me."

My accomplishments didn't relieve the unhappiness I carried inside because of my paralysis in the most intimate spheres. But Leah's company, even for those few minutes each day, began to brighten my world and give it color. For the first time I began to feel it *might* be possible for me to live all the dimensions of my being, no longer shadowed by shame.

Leah came to *me*— I'd been incapable of going to her. A pretty girl named Evelyn Mann, a few months before, had started smiling at me in journalism class. Every time I'd looked her way I'd seen her beaming at me. It was obvious that she was inviting my approach, and yet there was some line deep inside me I wasn't warrior enough to charge past. After a time her smile had disappeared like the sun going behind clouds.

I didn't know how to reach out further to Leah, either. But then, one Friday afternoon, we were walking to her math class, across the hall from my history class. I was carrying her books, having requested the honor as a jocular symbol of our friendship. As I gave them back to her, Leah asked, "Would you like to come over tomorrow night? 'The Bird Man of Alcatraz' is on TV."

I tried not to betray my excitement or my fear. Her eyes were gentle and caring. Would I know what to do when I got there, though? Who could be certain?

"Yes! Sure!" I finally managed to stammer out.

Crossing the hall to history class, I felt my own history to be on the verge of a revolution. I scarcely heard Mr. Wilson's lecture. *A girl had invited me to her house on a Saturday night!*

All my friends' stories came flooding back. Would Leah attack me? Would I be able to keep up a conversation? She said she just wanted to watch television. But suddenly I was about to do something I'd never done! Some rite of passage to a new life had presented itself, at least as a possibility.

2.

That rite of passage led through a ribbon of streets I knew pretty well, straight east a mile from our large, brick house by the tall, wrought-iron street light on the quiet corner of Waterman and Williams. It led down Waterman and across Big Bend Boulevard in the direction of the city of St. Louis. Parkview Place, where Leah's family lived, close to the Washington University campus, bordered on the city.

My parents had gone out on that cold Saturday evening and I was alone with my crippled grandmother, who lived with us. I showered at 7 p.m. in eager, nervous expectancy. Looking in the mirror while drying my hair, I noticed the fuzz that had lately been growing on my face. Decisively, if sneakily, I reached for my father's razor and the shaving cream. The bathroom suddenly seemed bathed in soft angel glow.

I emerged a few minutes later, toilet paper bits covering two small wounds I had opened in the blood-ritual of my first shave.

"You tried to *shave?*" my grandmother asked as I presented myself to her, dressed in my best sweater and my winter coat.

"Yes, 'Maw," I shyly admitted. A rare look of love and wisdom came into her eyes. I felt closer to her than I had since sitting on her bed as a small child, discussing "the poor Chinese" and other world problems.

"You're going to see Leah?" she asked. She still looked happy for me, but I felt embarrassed, and wondered if it had been wise to have told my parents where I was going.

Once out the door in the cold, purple-sky winter night, though, I was leaving all that had happened so far in my life back in the mythic, golden-lighted house behind me. Every room in that house bore the ghosts of my actions, words and thoughts. I'd been just five when we'd moved there.

In front of me, once I left the lighted sphere of the corner streetlight, there were only the purple sky, the black winter shadows of trees, some light snow dusting the ground, and the silent hulks of homes and dark cars. Pulling up the hood of my parka, I braved the ribbon of sidewalk before me —the path, perhaps, beyond boyhood.

My thoughts, accompanying me, whirled like the snow—thoughts of anticipation, still alloyed with a bit of anxiety. The unknown stretched ahead like the dark night I was cutting through with every step.

I crossed Big Bend, not going to Williams' Drugstore this time. No, I was going *past* all old landmarks, past everywhere I'd been before. Leaving behind the lions atop the stone pillars that guarded the entrance to Ames Place, I quickly covered the several blocks of that neighborhood. A grassy back trail led me into Parkview Place, with its carriage houses and the park in the median of its gated, private streets.

Across the park I could see Leah's house, bright porch beacon illumining white brick, bright red shutters and door. Only one home, amid the row of stately, sleeping structures, fit Leah's description. Could the light be burning for *me* and for me alone, I wondered with a touch of pride?

I rang the bell. A moment later, I heard sounds behind the oaken door and pulled on the handle of the glass storm door. After a moment of typical door-opening fumbling and air pressure resistance, Leah stood before me smiling, wearing a white sweatshirt and a dark, plaid skirt.

I stepped up the stone step from the porch to the living room, wondering what to say first. As I walked into the room, a great cry of many voices suddenly broke the silence of the room, pouring into my ears, vibrating my whole body. A hundred people seemed to leap out of woodwork, jump from behind chairs, fly from landings and chandeliers and kitchen.

"*Surprise!*" they all shouted. "*Surprise!*"

Faces of everyone I knew seemed to be approaching me from all directions—my friends from my club and their girlfriends, my friends from journalism class, my friends from the football team. How had Leah found out my birthday was next week? No one had ever given me a surprise party before! It was like being welcomed in heaven!

People stood around me, talking and laughing. After some time, greetings began to simmer down. The crowd slowly melted away. Music came on. People went back to their conversations, their eating. Couples on the couches began making out.

Finally, Leah alone stood beside me. She took my hand and led me over to a small sofa in front of the fireplace. She gave me a little push in the belly so that I'd sit down. Then, joining me on the sofa, she proceeded to give me a pert little kiss on my left cheek, and another one on my right.

Leah straightened up and sat beside me, smiling. I took her strongly in my arms and pressed my lips, eyes closed, fully and deeply into hers, into the lips and soul of this dear girl who had led me single-handedly to myself.

The Incident

1.

The sun still felt good as I walked back to my dorm from the Sergeant Hall cafeteria after dinner. I rested in my bed for a little while, then got up, changed clothes, and started walking towards the next driveway south—Tech Auditorium, where the big event was about to take place.

I was grateful spring had come, having felt myself fading away almost to nonexistence, trudging to classes through up to a foot of snow during the seemingly interminable Chicago winter. It was my first year away from home, and so far I'd been unable to make an emotionally healthy transition from my parents' hands-on doting. I'd joined a fraternity, but feeling out of place, had quit after two quarters. Now I spoke to almost no one and walked around as if a cone of isolation surrounded me. I was starting to think there might be something wrong with me.

Spring made the physical act of getting to classes easier, and the bright green of all the new leaves, along with the hundreds of crocuses that painted the campus with the school colors, purple and white, was cheering. An artist who called himself "Warmth" had begun drawing big yellow smiley-faces on the sidewalk fronting the campus along Sheridan Road. Every one of them I passed appeared as a personal challenge.

The big event I was heading to was a major policy speech by Senator Edward Kennedy—right on our campus. Rumor had it that at least part of his speech would be about the Vietnam War. The article in the *Daily Northwestern* had conjectured about whether members of SDS might start shouting, "Talk about the War, Senator!" one after another from various parts of the auditorium, as they'd recently done in Madison, Wisconsin.

I didn't know or care much about that. I simply intended to go because I wanted to be well-informed. I felt fortunate to be on a campus where national and even world leaders regularly came to give addresses. During the winter I'd seen speeches by King Hussein of Jordan and Eduardo Mondlane, leader of the guerilla movement in Mozambique.

Passing a stand of bushes and turning left into the Tech driveway, I caught my first glimpse of the scene outside the massive metal doors that led into the auditorium. I could see right away that I should have arrived 45 minutes before the scheduled beginning of the talk, instead of half an hour. The lobby was already thronged with people milling around or talking.

Entering the building through the propped-open doors, I found the admission line, already stretching three-fourths of the way back to where I stood. I planted myself behind the last person in line and immediately, someone new came and stood behind me. By the time I'd made my way up near the security man, I glanced back and saw the line winding all the way outside.

I bided my time as the two people still ahead of me went through the checkpoint. Finally, I stood face to face with a uniformed security man behind a wooden podium. The way in to the auditorium was cordoned off by velvet chains, and only a narrow pathway was open.

"Let's see your student ID," the chunky guard said. I reached into my back pocket and panicked. The pocket was empty.

"I left my wallet in my other pants, back in my dorm," I said, forcing my voice to sound calm. "I do go to school here, though. Can't you just let me in?"

"Go back and get it, and then come and show me," he said matter-of-factly.

"But the auditorium will be full by then!" I protested.

The Incident

The lobby was overflowing now, and there was scarcely room enough for everyone to stand. The din of the crowd was constant. I felt the swelling line physically pressing into me from behind. Then, suddenly—I have no idea how it happened—I found myself *grappling* with the man, who'd come out from behind his podium and was holding onto me. I was *fighting* to get away from him! Suddenly, I seemed to be in the wrong life! I, who had always been a peaceful person, who'd been in scarcely any fights even as a child, was being treated like a criminal!

"*Hey Rod, I've got one for you!*" the man shouted out, very loud. Who was Rod? Got one what? Couldn't someone slow all this down?

From somewhere inside the foyer, a little phalanx of burly, black-suited men came marching out. There were six of them. Was I hallucinating? Secret Police? Here in America? As I continued to struggle mentally and physically, the men grabbed me and sort of lifted me away from the checkpoint guard and began dragging me into the foyer. Half pushed, half carried, I saw again the throngs of colored-shirted, jabbering students filling the lobby. Only the very closest, the ones the men had to push their way through, even looked up.

Too disoriented to shout, I tried to use my feet as a brake. But there were too many of them. They bore me all the way inside the foyer, where fewer people could see us. Were they going to beat me—hurt me—now that we were out of sight? The little procession kept moving, bearing me to a deserted place at the side of the foyer. One of them pushed open a side door, and all together they roughly dumped me onto the floor outside the auditorium area. Someone pulled the door shut.

Suddenly, there was total quiet. Looking around, I saw that I sat on a green-tiled floor, alone in a deserted corridor of the building lined with lockers and classroom doors. I reached up and pulled on the brass handle of the door through which I'd been ejected. Locked. Oddly, from here I couldn't even hear the throng in the lobby or the pre-speech buzz inside the rapidly-filling hall. I felt roughed up, shocked, but—I quickly took bodily inventory—not physically injured. It was so peaceful out here that except for the fact that I would never on my own sit like this on the floor of a public building, what had taken place a moment ago seemed preposterous.

Yet it had happened. I felt like I was sitting at the bottom of a deep well. This was worse than a winter of slow humiliation. It was worse than walking to class in deep snow. It was even worse than having had the last girl I'd been out with, way back in September during Orientation Week, desert me in the middle of a song we were dancing to, after I'd leaned over to tell her something to make her laugh—shouting "You're crazy!" and walking away.

My self-pity alternated with rage now, as I replayed the expulsion in my head. It was as if I'd been carried away not by human beings but by a raw force, the men working in tandem to create something superhuman like one of the twisters that occasionally sped with unbelievable power through my home town, upturning everything in their path. My will, my intentions, meant nothing.

Suddenly, though, an impulse surged through my body and I stood up. No, I would *not* let them do this to me. I *would* recover my dignity. I pulled again on the door handle, this time as hard as I could. Then I made a fist, and began to knock hard upon the heavy wooden surface.

After a little while, the knocking hurt. You *had* to do it hard. If the auditorium was so soundproof that I couldn't hear anything inside, then no one inside could hear me, either, unless I *pounded*. The door became literally the doorway between me and everything I not only wanted, but *needed*. I kept up my pounding without stopping, soon learning that an extended palm can make as much noise as a fist, and two of them, even more!

By now, the senator's speech had no doubt begun. Well, if necessary, I would stay here at my post and keep doing this until it was over. After around ten minutes, however, the door opened. The shrewd, bird-like face of a bespectacled older gentleman peered at me from a few inches away as he leaned forward. He must have worked for the university. Possibly he was another undercover man, but he wore a brown, pin-striped suit, not one of those black uniforms. I had the sense he knew what had happened.

"Come in," he said in a kind, low voice, motioning with his head and briefly smiling. He walked away towards the back as soon I entered the auditorium. I found a vacant seat near a side aisle, only a few rows from the stage. It was at least as good a seat as if I'd come in at the beginning. Still, I couldn't tell you much of what Senator Kennedy said. My mind just kept replaying that unbelievable scene over and over, seeing the big, black, 12-footed dragon that had overpowered me.

As I left the auditorium, I began to realize that getting back in to see the speech was not enough. I needed an apology. The world, and especially the Northwestern student body, needed to know what kinds of things happened on this campus—what kind of thing could happen to them!

When the talk ended, I went home and typed up a narrative of the incident. Having been an editor of my high school paper, and being in fact a journalism student here at Northwestern, I knew how to write a news story. Immediately walking my article across campus to the *Daily Northwestern* office, I gave it to the person on night duty. I felt better then. I fell asleep shortly after returning home, satisfied that my expose' would alert the whole student body to the danger of this dark side of our prestigious university.

Searching the paper the next morning, however, I felt puzzled. My piece was not the lead article. I couldn't find it anywhere above the fold of the front page. Finally, though, near the bottom of the page, in small type, I found a headline: DIFFERING ACCOUNTS OF TECH

AUDITORIUM INCIDENT. "Campus Security Chief Rod Wilson and an NU freshman gave differing accounts of an incident that occurred at Tech Auditorium last night," the article began. It went on to quote the Chief saying, "If he'd been polite, we would have let him in." My "exposé" had ended up rewritten as a dispute between an important official and an "NU freshman" who did not even matter enough to be named in the lead.

I felt crushed and enraged! Instead of being vindicated, I had become the victim of a further humiliation. My very honesty and possibly my sanity were being called into question. No one was more polite and obsequious than I. Mother had drilled those qualities into me all through childhood. But the person I'd been, whose "politeness" had been a veneer even over acceptance of abuse—I was not going to be that person any longer.

2.

This budding springtime week of 1967 was also the second week of the campaign for Student Body President at Northwestern. Such an event might ordinarily have passed without arousing the slightest interest from an isolated campus atom like me. This year, however, the presidential race was attracting enormous campus-wide notice. Front-page banner headlines about it appeared in every edition of the *Daily*.

A student named Aldo Frank, a theatre major a year ahead of me who was a member of Theta Chi fraternity, had begun a campaign that he called Student Power, which did not stop with the usual Vote-For flyers and glad-handing. Instead, Frank's campaign featured daily marches through the streets of Evanston. Adherents carried signs supporting a proposed Fair Housing law in the university-dependent town, and others condemning the Vietnam War. After each march through town, the group snaked across the campus green to a landmark known as The Rock.

The Incident

Ordinarily, The Rock was simply something for fraternities to splash paint on and deface with graffiti before their party weekends. Frank, however, made it the site of daily campaign events he called "Bitch-Ins." First he, and then other students, one at a time, would ascend the painted boulder. Standing up there with an electric bullhorn in hand, the speaker would air grievances against the university. Every day a crowd of one to two hundred listeners, many of whom had also been marchers, assembled. Students angrily denounced dorm curfews, campus ROTC, university research that helped the war machine, Northwestern's complicity with racist housing and with South African apartheid. Such public outcries had previously been unheard of at our sleepy, conservative school, where in those days even the football team did not arouse much excitement.

I had seen the photos in the *Daily* of the crowds at The Rock. One day, while walking to a class, I'd seen the line of chanting, sign-carrying students march onto the campus after their jaunt through town. I hadn't known what to make of any of this. My father had been an active socialist during his own college days. I'd grown up in the era of Martin Luther King, when sign-carrying demonstrators had become American icons. But my life had been sheltered in suburbia. I had very little awareness even of King's greatness. In high school, I had regarded him from a distance as simply "a great orator." The phrase had seemed safe. I'd described Dr. King that way once at home, Dad had not corrected me. He hadn't given me a lecture about the moral *purpose* of such "oratory," and how it was only a means to an end, justice.

Suddenly, now, a vector had been drawn from these events in the world to my own newly deflowered life. It all became clear, the reason why people anywhere carried signs and took risks. They were voiceless people insisting that their voices finally be heard! Why hadn't I understood that before? Apparently, it was something no one could really explain in a history or current events course. You had to *hurt*, to understand. Now, for the first time, I got it.

3.

I'd occasionally had conversations with a couple of freshmen in my dorm who were political activists. One of them, Sam Linton, was so precocious that even as a freshman, he was president of the Northwestern chapter of Students for a Democratic Society. He always had answers to my questions; I liked that. Sometimes, though, he made statements that sounded patently outrageous. "The Peace Corps is just low-temperature napalm," he'd told me once.

My other activist acquaintance, Ricky Moses, was more level-headed. A lanky, good-looking Texan with wavy hair and an easy-going manner, Ricky was a freshman member of the Student Senate. A few days ago I'd read an article describing a speech he'd given supporting the Student Power movement. That evening I walked upstairs and down the hall, and knocked on the door of the room I knew to be his.

"Did I see your name in the paper today?" he drawled in a friendly voice when he saw me, his big eyes not even looking surprised to find me there.

"If you read to the very bottom of the article you did," I said with a sarcastic laugh. "I'm pissed off! Rod Wilson lied and said I wasn't polite! Six of them just came out of the shadows and carried me away like a violent offender, Rick—just for forgetting my student ID!"

"Might all this have something to do with this visit?" he asked smiling

"Well, I was hoping I could tell my story at the rally tomorrow. I know you're friends with Aldo Frank. I was wondering if you could talk to him for me."

"You should talk to him yourself," he said, and then thought for a minute. "Tell you what," he went on. "I'm meeting Aldo at the Grill tomorrow morning at 9. Why don't you join us?"

"I don't have a class till ten," I said. "I'll see you there!"

The next morning, holding a cup of coffee I'd just paid for, I scanned the busy Campus Grill. Finally, I found Moses sitting in a booth against the far wall with a person I recognized as Frank. Aldo was tall, but slightly pale and not at all athletic-looking, and wore a sport coat. If I hadn't known which was the leader, I would have picked Moses.

"Rick!" I shouted as I got near. Moses nudged Aldo and pointed in my direction, and they both stood up as he introduced me. We shook hands. They slid into one side of the booth and I, pushing my coffee ahead of me, into the other.

Aldo smiled and looked at me in a friendly way. "Rick was just telling me what happened the other night. I'd seen the article, but apparently it didn't tell the whole story."

"That's right," I said. "I didn't do anything to provoke them. It was kind of an accident, and then all of a sudden they were treating me like an assassin."

"Well, here's the thing about the Bitch-Ins," Aldo said. "I don't stage-manage them. They really are spontaneous. People just go up there and say whatever they want. I hear your passion about this, and I can understand how you'd feel put down by the article. If you're at the Rock, of course you're welcome to tell your story. Student Power's really about just that."

I joined the march through town that afternoon. I *enjoyed* every step of it: seeing the scorn on the faces of a group of ladies about to enter the Orrington Hotel as we passed by; the irritation of two businessmen who looked up from some contract they were going over outside an office building. They all acted like "grown-ups," with us as their uncontrollable teenage kids. But a bus driver flashed a two-finger V sign at us. A cleaning lady waiting for the bus smiled at us. For once I felt I was looking at the world from the *right* side. And it felt good bonding with the other marchers, as we sang: *"Ain't gonna let nobody turn me around…"*

4.

As we approached the Rock, another fifty or so people waiting for us broke into a cheer. A TV camera pointed at us. A sense of thrill worked its way up from somewhere inside me. The line of marchers broke up and began re-forming around the landmark, painted orange this week with the Greek letters Sigma Chi all over it. Aldo began his climb. Someone handed him the bullhorn when he reached the top.

"Thank you, to those of you who joined today's march," he began graciously. He had a Texas twang like Ricky, I realized, though not as pronounced. "Tomorrow we'll march again! We'll keep marching. We'll march until there is justice in America! Until the War is over and our university's resources are no longer being used to burn people alive and suppress popular movements abroad!" The crowd roared.

"Now, some people ask whether student politics should have anything to do with war or racism. Let's ask them whether college should have anything to do with life! This university is part of the war machine, part of the racism machine. And we are *citizens* on this campus! We have a *responsibility* to take our stand! That is what Student Power means!"

A loud voice in the rear shouted "Right on!"

"And we're not alone. A couple of weeks ago, 400,000 people marched in New York City to end the war. A month ago right here in Chicago, Martin Luther King, Jr. led a march of five thousand for peace. He knows racism can't end unless the war ends. All over the country, in rallies just like this one on other campuses, *our* voices are starting to be heard—and they *must* be heard!"

"And now, it is time for *your* voices to be heard. This is about free speech, as much as it is about anything else. One of our great universities was ground to a halt, a couple of years back, all for the right to free speech that we exercise here today!"

"Who has something to say?"

Standing near the front of the crowd, I raised my hand. Frank beckoned for me to come up. I strode forward to the foot of the Rock and waited until he had climbed down. Then I put my hand to one of the rough stone outcroppings, found a foothold in an indentation, and began to climb. I discovered another foothold a few feet up, and boosted myself toward the top. Holding on up there with one hand to the cold, smooth rock, I reached out with the other for the bullhorn that Aldo held up toward me.

I steadied myself, taking a deep breath and looking out over the crowd of students, teaching assistants, even a few Professors. My history teacher, Mr. Weld, stood near the back in his tie and white shirt. Ricky Moses stood next to Aldo. Off to one side I noticed John Barnes, a wraith-like hippie who lived in our dorm. The camera from the local TV station was pointing its eye straight at me. The afternoon sky was like a blue explosion. The air felt warm on my skin, but not too warm. I could practically feel the spring sap rising everywhere, as I began: "The other night I went to Tech Auditorium hear Senator Kennedy…"

I had not rehearsed my speech. Still powered by the rage engendered by my humiliation, I felt confident in this friendly crowd that my public speaking experience from as far back as a sixth grade recitation of the Gettysburg Address on Lincoln's birthday, would sculpt my raw passion and carry me through.

"Rod, I've got one for you!" I quoted the Security man loudly. "Rod," I said, "turned out to be a thug!" As I visualized the heavy, black-

suited men and the rough way I'd been treated, that word came naturally. Before me, heads bobbed sympathetically.

By the time I got to the part of the story that took place after I'd been thrown out the door, I was actually enjoying myself, feeling relaxed enough to improvise a bit stylistically: *"I wasn't going to take it!"* I shouted. *"I began knocking on the door as hard as I could! I knocked in waltz time! I knocked in Calypso! I knocked in Soul!"* I went on to narrate the whole story, including being made into an anonymous "NU Freshman" in the Daily.

"And I'm telling all this at a Student Power rally because my story makes it clear that we need Student Power in order for you to be safe here, on your own campus! So you can walk around without getting roughed up by people who are supposed to be here to protect you! So that your word will not be rendered impotent by your own campus newspaper! Vote for Aldo Frank!"

I stepped down to strong, prolonged applause and a few loud cheers. "Tell 'em, Marty!" a voice near me shouted. I looked up to see Mike Chekov, a senior business major from my former fraternity whom I'd always respected, *beaming* at me from under his Harris tweed sport coat and designer hair. I smiled back as I passed him. I handed the bullhorn back to Aldo, who flashed his own *huge* smile of appreciation.

The crowd began to break up, and I began walking back to my dorm. As I was about to go inside, a loud, breathless voice called my name. I turned. A tall, rather strange fellow named Jake von Bell was approaching me at almost a run. He lived on the 3rd floor. Sometimes he sat in the lobby with a guitar, always singing the same song, whose chorus went, *"And I can't help but wonder where I'm bound..."*

"Marty!" he said again, catching up. "Hey, if they didn't require student IDs, anybody could get in! Even a guy who wanted to shoot a Senator!"

The Incident

I looked back at Jack, his raincoat, his pimpled face. I'd been so glib, a few minutes ago. Now I couldn't think of a logical answer.

"What happened to me was wrong, Jack. That's all I know." He shrugged, and I walked past him into the dorm, and up to my room. I was thankful that my roommate was out. I needed to be alone.

I thought back through all that had happened. Could it only have been two days? That guy who had trudged so sullenly through the winter. He had been trudging toward all this, without knowing. Now I'd bonded in the streets with other students. I'd allied myself with a worldwide movement. The spring tide was heady. The very trees seemed to be whispering in the breeze, "Change, *Change!*" All over the world we, the new generation, were going to overturn the Old Order.

But more importantly, when pushed to the edge, I'd seen myself fight back. Regardless of what Jake believed, that was the crux of the matter for me. Now I knew there was somebody inside me who wanted *life*!

SUMMER OF '68

Part One: Tunnel

1.
Coming back from the lake, we re-entered the St. Louis metro area on St. Charles Rock Road. I was in the back seat next to Elise, my beautiful, blonde new girlfriend. Both her parents in front seemed older than my own. Her father was driving. He had a roofing business, Elise had told me.

Crossing I-270 and then Lindbergh Boulevard, the car entered St. Ann and my contentment yielded to the feelings I always had on this route through the county. The hodge-podge of asphalt, strip malls, featureless office buildings and shopping centers without a whiff of aesthetic or even a plan, seemed to be closing in on me. Life suddenly seemed hopeless, its possibilities nil.

I'd been raised a mere 10 or so miles away in a world of shady trees, parks, large brick homes and a bastion of culture called Washington University. Nearby was Clayton, with its much more stylish business center, as well as the up-to-date library where Mother worked. Then came Ladue, the wealthy suburb where the modern ranch homes and even mansions were hidden by forest-like stands of trees, vines and bramble. Driving west on Ladue Road, you seemed to be in uninterrupted Nature, until it dawned on you that this was an example of what money could buy.

I sat back and tried to be patient. St. Ann passed and my contentment returned. I gave Elise's hand a squeeze. The summer was turning out a million times better than had seemed possible when I'd returned home after my sophomore year at Northwestern, a mere month ago.

2.

I'd come back a wreck. My light had gone out months before. There was scarcely any way to hide the truth from my parents now, as I'd tried to do during our weekly phone calls throughout the school year. I had no clue how to rekindle the light, or if it could even be done.

It all had to do with love, of course. I'd met someone in the fall at a forum where my apartment-mate Bernie and other student leaders were discussing the student movement. The past spring, we at Northwestern had joined our compatriots all over the world in mounting campus demonstrations. The feeling as the new '67-8 academic year began was: *you ain't seen nothin' yet!*

I wasn't a leader, but I was friends with leaders, and I wrote for the semi-underground newspaper we'd started, the Real Press. I felt like a semi-celebrity: *much* closer to the vortexes of energy and action than I'd been most of the year before. Back then, I'd practically fallen through a hole in the Earth. An incident in which I'd been roughed up by campus security had wounded my ego so badly that it had lit a fire in, resulting in a new identity as a radical. I exulted in this. I loved answering people's question, "What are you?"—meaning I guess, Democrat, Republican or whatever—with "I'm a *Radical!*" Sometimes I could see the asker cower. There was power in the word, even a vague feeling of smoke from an anarchist bomb that might be lurking in my shoulder bag.

This sense of identity enabled me to talk to the pretty, dark-haired girl who was jostled up against me in the crowd as the forum adjourned for socializing. I'd ended up inviting her to dinner the coming Saturday. With the help of a few tokes of hashish, we'd gone into my tiny bedroom at our clapboard Maple Street apartment a few blocks from campus. There, I'd discovered I'd hooked a tiger! Not only was she attractive, she also meant business in bed! She clawed, scratched and screamed when I touched her. Her passion was a thrill, but also a problem—*my God, if she's this intense, she's going to need me to go all the way!*

I didn't know if I was capable of that. In spite of having had steady girlfriends since junior high, my experience was limited to kissing and at most, heavy necking. I believed I'd had several wet dreams, but my conscious manhood had been delayed somehow, probably by something that had happened in childhood. I might even know what it was, but everything inside was very dark and murky, and I felt under the spell of some taboo. There were moods and fantasies that came on me at times and brought out "someone else," yet I walled off the whole messy business as much as I could. As far as actually encountering a woman sexually—would I ever be able to do that?

In spite of being unsure of the road to sexual wholeness, I sensed it was time to move along on the journey. I'd returned to campus this year as Northwestern sales rep for Portal Publications, which printed the West Coast rock concert posters with their psychedelic art and lettering. I was intrigued by them, and it had occurred to me that selling them could be the equivalent of a part-time job. I'd written the company and had received a catalogue and exclusive rights to take orders in the dorms. It never really came to much, financially, but thumbing through the catalogue one day I'd seen an ad for a poster titled "Yab-Yum." The poster showed a naked woman astride a naked man, the two of them surrounded by a pink, paisley background.

Up to this point in my life, I'd have been far too inhibited to ever order such a thing. Now I did. When it arrived, I hung it on my bedroom wall. I felt, somehow, that I was calling such experiences into my life. It hadn't been long before they'd showed up.

As our relationship and our love-making progressed, my girlfriend took to saying in a hushed, bedroom whisper, *"You're insatiable!"* At first I took that as a compliment. However, slowly I began to realize that what she meant was that a man as aroused as I was usually had an orgasm.

I couldn't tell her the truth. She had told me once, in response to my query, that she was a virgin. I'd said nothing about my own past, but tried to "act experienced," whatever that meant. My act was a wash. Insatiable: how could I become "satiable"?

One night several weeks into our relationship, I was studying for my first economics test. I'd signed up for the course believing it behooved someone in the New Left to know *something* about that subject. I faced many hours with the textbook, having gotten very little from the lectures or the chapters I'd previously tried to read. After a while, still finding the prose deadly, I retreated to bed, propping myself up against the wall with pillows, and tried to continue.

I found myself dallying almost vacantly with my penis with one hand, gently stroking it as I read. I drifted away from the book into a fantasy, and suddenly, from deep inside, felt a mighty force rising unexpectedly! It took me a moment to even realize what it was. Like an ocean tide, it kept rising and rising. No wonder this force held such a central place in human consciousness! Finally, it exploded out the tip of my penis and a stream of whitish liquid shot several inches into the air! The stuff continued to pour and pour out, accompanied by the most intensely pleasurable feelings I'd ever experienced.

After a surprising length of time, the electric thrill slowly subsided. I lay spent upon my bed, a dazed, happy expression on my face, my book face-down on my chest. Its cover was a little wet. Who cared? Arriving at the classroom later that morning, I could still feel the tingling in my crotch. It made me smile. All anxiety about the economics test had vanished. In the night, I had passed a much greater test.

I smiled again every time I thought of the unlikely way in which I'd "discovered my manhood." As good as any other way! Although I still didn't know the precise mechanics of "how to do it" with an actual woman, I felt that, now, would take care of itself. That very night, I wet the bed and both our bodies with another mighty surge. No more whispers of "insatiable." I, *we,* were off and running!

There followed three months of intense cocooning in that bedroom—even skipping morning classes together sometimes to make love. It was as if I'd lived in some cardboard world until now, and suddenly had travelled with her as guide through a jungle, to the outer wall of an ivory Temple. We'd entered the Temple together. Who cared what the rest of the world had to offer? It was nothing compared to this! The cardboard world could collapse in ruins and decay, for all I cared.

Winter break came. My lover and I returned to our respective hometowns. Hers was in Marin County, California, across the bay from San Francisco. Writing her a passionate letter every day, I began to feel concern when no replies had arrived after nearly a week. Was the mail getting delivered? Had I gotten the right address? Each day I continued to wait for the mailman like a faithful dog in the front hall of our house. When I heard the *clink* of the metal box on the ivy-covered brick wall outside, I expectantly opened the heavy oak door, only to meet disappointment yet again.

3.

Back on campus, my worst fears were realized. My beloved told me she'd reunited with her high school boyfriend. Not only that, but though he was 2,000 miles away again, she wanted to see me less. Sometimes now on a Friday night, she stayed in the dorms to visit her friend Don, a boy who had such huge problems, she said, that he was seeing a psychiatrist. I commiserated with her in sympathy for poor Don, and yet it seemed her spending time with him, whatever they were doing, was part of the leaking away of my very *raison d'être.*

A week or two after our return to the campus, we went to see the movie everyone was talking about, *The Graduate.* I sat spellbound, taking in the lush scenes of Berkeley and the Big Sur coast. I felt awed that this creature beside me had actually grown up near there! Midway through the film I leaned over and whispered in her ear, *"I want to come and live with you in your magic city by the bay!"*

She looked straight ahead and whispered, loudly enough for me to hear: *"I've left you."*

When the film was over, I drove us back to my place. Bernie, my apartment mate, was out as usual. The two of us smoked a joint and went into my bedroom. I'm certain that the next vignette took place in that very bedroom. Yet every time I picture it in my mind, the backdrop I see is some hardscrabble dive with windows fronting on a freight yard!

Eyeing her as she sat on the edge of my bed in her very becoming salt-and-pepper dress, I thought of those dagger words, "I've left you." And yet here she was! As if to prove that, I reached out, took her in my arms, and embraced her tightly. She allowed me to do so. But though I had her body firmly in my embrace, I knew I did not have *her*! There was absolutely nothing I could do to have *her*, ever again.

The paradox was unbearable! I withdrew my arms and simply sat on the chair near the bed and looked at her once again, hating myself for not being *enough*! Clenching both fists, I began to pound my chest, and then my head, as hard as I could. I had failed. It was *my* fault I didn't have what she wanted.

After a time, I stopped hitting myself and looked at her again. Once more, I heard her words in my mind and reached out to try to prove them false. Again, the effort was futile and I turned my redoubled rage on myself.

After three rounds of this, she rose and walked to the door of our rear-entrance apartment, then out onto the porch. Bathed in moonlight, she descended the wooden steps to the backyard, continuing around to the front sidewalk. I remained alone with my grief and self-pity.

And yet, we *had* been lovers. Fate arranged one more meeting. I no longer remember whether one of us phoned the other that Saturday night, in the dead of winter, or whether we "ran into each other" walking along Lake Michigan beside its natural wonder, the great white waves that appeared to have been flash-frozen in mid-leap toward shore.

We walked back to my place together and I lit some candles. Then we made the most gentle, perfect love, in perfect silence, a true lovers' farewell.

4.

That night was not a reversal, however. It was more a moment out of time. After that, she no longer returned my calls, and I soon stopped trying. It was months later, in the spring, when I saw her next. We passed one another one morning in the student grill and stopped to talk briefly. I found it hard to relate. Wearing shorts, she seemed skinnier than I remembered—partly the person I'd known, partly someone else.

I remained tormented. I still lived in my white Temple. The whiteness of my symbol had been her flesh. I lived there like a twin whose womb-mate has died. Her memory haunted my every moment. Her shadow seemed everywhere, but she was nowhere.

I was still enrolled as a full-time student, with hundreds of pages each week to read for my literature courses alone. I had a job during dinner hour washing pots at an Italian restaurant around the corner from the apartment. I still tried to help with the Real Press, but I was pathetically unable to concentrate. Sometimes I skipped a morning class, the way she and I had done together, and went back home to the locus of our former love rituals, just to lie in bed alone.

When the weather turned warm, I found a partial refuge. I would take my books and go sit on a park bench along the strip of green that ran beside the lake south of campus. I wasn't successful at my efforts to keep up with reading assignments, but the grass, trees, lake and sky, especially that magical, healing green, brought a relative calming. As long as I was there, on what I called "my island," I survived.

As spring progressed, I encountered a bearded poet, an acquaintance who'd just been jilted by *his* girlfriend. We began to commiserate. Once he even came to my island of green, sat on the bench beside me, and railed about his former lover, the capitalist system, and any number of other things. My bench seemed to have become a pirate ship that day.

Another time the two of us visited a friend of his, a Czech student named Hruska, who lived in a rooming house. From Hruska's record player, a voice wailed with a pain I recognized. My poet friend and I examined the album cover. On the back was a strange painting of a woman with her wrists chained, looking at and reaching up through bright orange flames. The front of the album had a grainy sepia photo of a rather handsome man, and the words: *Songs of Leonard Cohen.*

5.

I passed my courses somehow, distinguishing myself in only one of them. I'd been excited about taking an advanced seminar in short story writing. My first effort was a stream-of-consciousness piece about—what else?—*her*. The teacher, a diminutive young man with thick glasses and a pock-marked face, gave me a B, commenting that my language was musical but the piece was too subjective to be called a story. I had another major story to go and was simply out of commission as far as being able to write at all on any other subject.

But among the campus politicos and eccentrics who would drop by our place was a certain grad student who happened to show up that week. This handlebar-mustachioed fellow always carried a beige leather pouch with him. All present would gather around the kitchen table during his visits, to watch him pour out its contents and announce their colorful names. He had a loud, affected voice like a hippie train conductor: *"Black African ganja!"* or *"Ammmmmyl nitrate!"*

The week my story was due, his voice declared *"Pure crystal meth!"* Though the idea of taking speed made me anxious, I knew it was my only chance at successfully completing the assignment. I bought some, licked it down, and soon felt like Superman. Several hours later I had written, longhand, a complete story about the world my high school friends and I had inhabited on weekend nights: our rivalry with another group, driving around in my convertible and our adventures "pool-hopping" in the wee hours. Its mood was a little like the movie *American Graffiti* that came out a few years later. By the time I'd finished typing it up, my system felt totally drained. I slept almost a whole day and night. But I got it in on time.

When I met with the teacher for our last conference, he spoke like an elder performing an initiation. "This piece is wonderful," he said. "I'm giving you an A for the course!" I sensed he knew how important it was to me to succeed at something, at this point in my life.

Even in this dark night, there was *something* to receive, to be proud of, to build on.

Part Two: Mandala

1.

On a sunny, hot day in June, I walked down the sidewalk on Maple Street for the last time, weighed down by a suitcase in one hand and a full duffel bag slung over a shoulder. Spring quarter was over and I had decided never to return to Northwestern. Two years had been enough. I'd discovered an identity, only to learn that a political identity was not sufficient to sustain me through lost love. I still did not know how to recover my wholeness, or if that was even possible—only that I would never voluntarily return to this place.

Back in St. Louis, my dad soon sensed my being out of sorts and sent me to a psychiatrist for an evaluation. I was supposed to resume a business partnership with him that had been very lucrative the previous summer, but begged off for a week or two, telling him I needed a little more time to rest.

By my second week in town I was still living aimlessly: reading, walking and driving around while trying to think of a way to postpone responsibilities further. One afternoon, I was walking home from the library along Washington, a shady, doglegged street that ran parallel to our own, two blocks north. Passing the home of a pair of twins I'd gone through the public schools with, I noticed a blonde head up on the porch. A moment later that head shouted my name and a lean dancer's body appeared, running down the steps to meet me.

"When did you get home?" she asked excitedly, taking my outstretched hands.

"About a week ago. You?"

"Two weeks. And I'm not going back to Wisconsin next year. I'm taking a year off. I may have a job in a hospital."

"I'm not going back to Northwestern, either."

"What are you going to do?"

"Transfer, I guess. But I haven't decided where."

"How are you spending your summer?"

"I'm supposed to work with Dad again. Probably start next week. But so far I'm just taking it easy. I had a tough spring."

"Me, too," she said.

I was silent, not wanting to speak more about my own state. Should I ask why *her* spring had been tough?

"Here we are around the corner from each other again," Elise went on. "Remember that summer just before college, when you gave us a ride in your ice cream truck?" We both smiled.

"After all those years as neighbors," I said, "I finally started getting to know the Hallwell twins, just as we were all about to move away." We both fell silent a moment. I thought of how our friendship had developed further, freshman year. The pledge class of my fraternity, from which I'd deactivated soon after, had gone to visit the Madison chapter. Knowing Elise was in school there, I'd phoned her and snuck away to meet her at a campus tavern. We'd talked for several hours. It was the closest I'd felt to anyone since leaving for college.

As we stood there now, an idea floated through my head. "Hey," I said. "I noticed that the cherries in my parent's backyard are ripe. If somebody doesn't pick them, the birds will. Why don't you come over some time and we can do it together! They're sour ones, OK to eat but *really* good in pies."

"I'd like to," she said. "My mom might even want to make a pie or two." Elise's mother had been an English war bride and their home looked a bit like a country cottage in the midlands.

"What day would be good?" I asked.

"Hmmm. I have another interview at the hospital tomorrow morning. After that I'm free, though. How about two o'clock?"

"Perfect," I said. "See you then!" I left feeling cheered. At least now in my dark tunnel, there was one thing to look forward to.

2.

At five before two the next day I sat on our front porch, legs dangling down, with a large, white plastic bowl on my lap. I saw Elise come into view walking down Williams Avenue, which connected our two streets. She waved her arm and smiled. Waving back and grasping the bowl at my side, I stood up to welcome her.

Her long strides quickly crossed the street to my parents' corner house. She followed me through the arched wooden gate with its peeling white paint and rusting handle, to the backyard. As I pushed it open it scraped the sidewalk, which led into the yard through a narrow passageway between our house and the fence to the Morgans' property next door. We passed the pink-and-white patio from whose center rose what remains the largest catalpa tree I've ever seen, with its yearly popcorn flowers in full bloom. The cherry tree, speckled pink with fruit, stood across a neglected lawn, beside a black fence that looked down onto a winding, sunken driveway with high cement walls. A few starlings squawked in the upper branches of the tree.

I handed Elise my bowl and climbed up into the tree, then motioned for her to give the bowl back. After wedging it into the crotch between two large, leafy branches, I extended a hand and helped her up. It had been an easy climbing tree even when I was a kid. I started picking cherries and dropping them in the bowl. Standing on another branch across the tree, Elise saw my technique and began to do her own picking.

We labored silently. The branches were drooping with fruit. The bowl filled up quickly. She had climbed a little higher than I had now. I looked up at her just as she looked down at me, and we both laughed.

The sun's rays filtered gently through the canopy of leaves. "Wow, it's a little green world up here!" Elise exclaimed.

"Isn't it beautiful? I tell you though, this wasn't as much fun when I did it alone last year. By the way, I almost forgot to ask—how was your interview this morning?"

"I think I've got the job. It's in the lab. Most of what I'll do—there's no delicate way to say it—is analyze stool samples!"

"That sounds like fun!" I laughed.

"I'll be a microbiologist! I've been getting interested in science lately."

"You're not going to be a dancer? Weren't you majoring in dance?"

"Yes, and I've started taking classes with a teacher I like here, too. But I don't think I'll ever go to New York or anything."

"Why not?"

"I'm not sure I love it enough. My sister loves both dance and theatre. She *has* to be doing at least one of them. I'm not sure it's quite that way for me."

"I might be starting to love writing that way," I mused shyly. "I wrote a short story at Northwestern that the teacher raved about."

"I'd like to read it," she said. "Weren't you majoring in journalism?"

"I transferred into English."

"You've always been a writer," she said. "I remember your column in the *Tom-Tom*."

"Lord! I feel embarrassed to think about that!" I replied. "This story's different. Confidentially, I actually took speed to write it. I wouldn't have been able to do it otherwise, considering the state I was in."

"Some of my friends have used diet pills to study. It's tempting," she said.

"I don't ever want to get near the stuff again," I agreed. "It's too powerful! Half an hour after licking up the powder, I became a genius. I could see all of literature, the whole history of the English language. Every sentence I wrote would start at the very beginning of history—maybe even the beginning of Creation. And there were allusions to all the authors I'd been studying. One paragraph would be in the style of Lawrence; the next one would imitate Joyce."

"What was the story about?" she asked.

"About high school—the guys I used to go around with on Saturday nights. How we'd find a kind of freedom sneaking into rich people's swimming pools in Ladue. How we were seeking freedom, but those nights were about the only times I ever really felt free. And about the rivalry between our group and the Marquees, remember them? I was desperately jealous of their fast cars, beautiful girls and general cool. I'm proud of the story, but it still left me wondering whether I'm really a writer or whether it was just the drug."

"I don't think it could have been *just* the drug, I mean, you could give methamphetamine to plenty of people, and they wouldn't come up with great short stories."

"I think you're right," I said. "But I have to *know*! It's still basically the only thing I've written that has any merit. I got inspired after Allen Ginsberg came to Northwestern, and started writing verse. Nothing I'd show anyone now, but at least I was trying. Well, enough about that. Did you have a boyfriend at Wisconsin?"

"Sort of. For a while. There was a German fellow, he used to always tell me *'You are a nymph of der voods!'* But it didn't really go anywhere. He was in love with an image."

All the time we'd been talking, we had continued picking cherries. Now, the bowl was full. I picked it up gently, cradled it against my breast, and climbed down from the tree. Then I took Elise's hand and helped her down. We both stood on the ground again, but the ground was different now. My legs felt as if they were growing up from it, anchored like they, themselves, were solid, healthy trees. The dark tunnel had vanished. The world was green and I was solidly in it.

Elise stood before me, smiling. We took each other's hands. Looking into one another's eyes, in awe of the transformative mystery that we had innocently entered in the green branches of my parents' tree, we moved toward one another and kissed.

Part Three: Art and Business

1.

Our pattern of connection began to evolve. During the days, we pursued our separate needs and interests. Around dinner time, one of us would phone the other, and we usually ended up getting together. I remained resurrected, out of the tunnel. There *was* life after lost love.

One night, Elise had something else to do. I went for a drive in the city alone, listening to the radio and seeing how things had changed there since I'd last been in town. Coming up Olive Street in midtown, I suddenly found myself amid the remnants of Gaslight Square, a neighborhood that had been alive with beatnik coffeehouses, restaurants and bistros as recently as my first departure for college. Jack Kerouac had even set a chapter of *On The Road* there. My parents had taken my brother and me to the best-known cabaret, the Crystal Palace, to see the Smothers Brothers on my 12th birthday.

Now, Gaslight Square had the look of a bombed-out city. Piles of rubble lay everywhere. The mock-ancient columns in front of Smoky Joe's Grecian Terrace, all boarded up now, had become real ruins. Even though Dad had mentioned on the phone once that a tourist had been murdered nearby and people had felt unsafe and stopped coming, it was a shock to see.

Soon after passing the Boyle Street intersection where activity had been centered, I was surprised to feel myself overcome with emotion. I felt a need to write. My hand was actually quivering. Pulling over to the curb, I got a notebook and pen out of my bag, flicked on the car's inside light, and began to scrawl line after fluent line of free-form verse until the cloud of feeling had finally been released.

Reading the page over, I was pleased to discover that the vivid contrast between the past and present of Gaslight Square had become a broader symbol: the poem was an elegy for an absent Mother. Begun in relation to the surroundings, the verse had dipped into the vat of my own internal grief. I *had* a mother, but emotionally it seemed there were places, losses, in me that I didn't know. I felt deeply satisfied with the piece as a poem. As I closed the notebook, a particularly pleasing line echoed through my mind: *"since your great hip shook itself to sleep."*

Driving home, I pondered. The muse had now visited twice, yet there was no telling when this sensitivity would come again. It wasn't the kind of thing you could wrestle to the ground and order to produce. It spoke on its own terms. It seemed, though, that my short story had *not* been a fluke or a mere drug-induced experience. Although this piece was verse and that one prose, they had been drawn from the same well.

I couldn't wait to type up the poem and read it to Elise.

2.

As Dad always reminded me—well, in his own words, "Son, there's a *practical* side to life!" He'd suddenly accosted me verbally when I was home for spring break in my freshman year, during the intermission of a play our family had gone to downtown. In reply to something I'd said, he'd looked at me with an expression of disgust and half-shouted, *"You're a dreamer! You live in a dream world!"*

I can see now that he had some awareness of how helpless I felt away from home. I also know he'd been a dreamer himself once. He'd wandered around America and Mexico as a young man. After the war, he'd wanted to go to film school on the GI Bill and get more training in camera work, editing, or even acting. He'd done some acting in Los Angeles before the war and worked with film in the Army Signal Corps. During their engagement, Mother had said she'd go back to California with him. At the last minute, she got cold feet. I was already born then and Dad refused to abandon his family, but he was stuck in St. Louis for years in jobs he hated.

It was a bit more complicated than that, but those were the bare facts. Now it seemed that if he couldn't be a dreamer, no one else could, either.

The previous summer, Dad had gotten me active in "practical life." When a loading dock job he'd found me had fallen through at the last minute, he'd asked whether I might be willing to help him with a little business he wanted to start. By now he was an assistant property manager at a huge apartment complex. It was the first job he really liked, after years in the family furniture store and more years pounding the pavement selling linoleum and carpet. He'd conceived the idea of a St. Louis Area Apartment Guide, a booklet that could be easily mailed or handed out at corporate or government offices. Every city has one today.

Dad may or may not have been the first person to ever think of the idea, but St. Louis had certainly never had anything of the kind before.

He needed someone to make the rounds of the many apartment complexes in the area and explain the concept: how we would send the booklets to large corporations, chambers of commerce, the armed forces and such places, and then anyone who rented an apartment from the Guide would earn us a $50 commission from management. It was a simple but flawless plan. Indeed, it ended up putting me through my second year at Northwestern.

Furthermore, our neighbor Eddie Hanniken was a printer, and Dad knew Eddie could do the book for a fraction of what retail printing would cost. There was a caveat: Eddie was an alcoholic who sometimes disappeared on long binges. But Dad believed he could "sit on him" and make him get the job done.

So I'd spent much of the summer of '67 in a sport coat and tie, carrying a briefcase filled with our contracts and publicity materials, driving the metro area from Mehlville in the south to Florissant in the north, and from the Mississippi River to West County. Many of the compounds' themes embodied a touch of fantasy. I visited a Japanese-style complex with a tea garden; one with pretend London Townhouses that had British flags flying everywhere; modern high-rises built alongside old churches in the central city; a number of "California-style" developments; and the big one where Dad worked, where all the streets were named after birds.

The results were remarkable! I signed up a large percentage of the owners and managers. It was almost too obvious that when these men saw the young go-getter I appeared to be—they saw themselves! Given that and the fact that the booklet really did make perfect economic sense, we had enough signed contracts to print and distribute even before I went back to Northwestern.

Eddie came through with flying colors, and the finished project looked good. I delivered stacks to the St. Louis Chamber of Commerce, plus the HR departments of McDonnell Aircraft, Monsanto, Budweiser, and a whole list of other places. The back cover featured a gorgeous photo of Mansion House Center, consisting of three glass-and-steel riverfront high-rises perfectly framed by the Gateway Arch.

3.

There's a crazy little side story about Mansion House's participation. I'll tell it because it sheds light on my family and its values.

The company signed our contract on my second visit. When I arrived at their top-floor office for a third time, it was just to pick up their artwork. However, as I sat in the waiting room John Cox, the tall, white-haired Texan who was personal secretary to the Executive Director, appeared and said, "Mr. Ashton would like to speak with you."

That was a surprise! Thus far, Mr. Cox had been the proxy for the company and we'd conducted all our business in his office. Now, I was ushered into his boss's inner sanctum. Paul Ashton, a bulky, well-dressed man with sharp eyes and a shiny bald head, rose from his desk to meet me as I came in, and shook my hand firmly.

"I love your verve and enthusiasm!" he said when we were both seated. "John has told me all about it. But there are limits to what you can accomplish with the tools available to you. I would like you to seriously consider working with us on your project. We have access to the very latest market research platforms. We could accomplish things together that you'd never dream of."

It sounded good. My parents were *wild* with excitement that night when I told them. We even drank a toast at dinner. We were like a stage family whose protégé has been discovered.

It took us only another week to realize that, preposterous as the idea may sound, Ashton and his big-shots were trying to swindle us out of our fledgling business! Some papers I was given to sign constituted a thinly-veiled attempt to steal the enterprise.

We quickly ended our dealings with Mansion House, though their ad remained as the booklet's handsome back cover. My parents accepted their middle-class status once more, and I no longer saw dollar signs staring back every time I looked in their eyes. (Frankly, my own eyes had not been exempt, either.) During the next year, Dad sent me a newspaper article telling how Ashton had been indicted for embezzling company funds, and had been sentenced to a prison term.

4.

After Elise and I got together, the light inside me shone brightly again. I told Dad I was ready to go to work on the second edition of the Guide. It was, after all, a golden goose: a summer's work, and it had gone on laying its eggs all year long.

But wouldn't you know—it wasn't the same! Dad had a way of speaking to people close to him sometimes as if he owned them. As a boy I'd helped him move furniture, which he rented to tenants, into their apartments at the same development he now helped manage. He often vented his frustration, as we carried a clumsy sofa together up a winding staircase, by shouting abuse at me. His invectives featured many repetitions of the word "stupid"—words that probably still affect my sense of self-worth.

When I'd been little, he would light up whenever he saw me, and that pure love remains one of my great inspirations. His disappointments over time, as well as the increasing complexity of parenting my brother and me as we grew older, became, I felt, the reasons for his shortening fuse.

In the summer of 1968, people around the world were declaring their freedom from situations of former servitude. A mere two days after I reported for work, as I was loading my briefcase, Dad shouted, *"No, not that way, stupid! Be careful, will you ever learn?"* I screamed back,

"Listen, I'm not taking your shit this year! Treat me like a human being or I'm out of here!" I stuffed my material in the briefcase and drove away.

When something similar happened a few days later, I shouted *"I quit!"* I left the briefcase at the house and drove straight to the swimming pool behind my friend Michael's house, a few blocks away. Climbing out of the car, I ripped the tie off my neck and hurled the symbol of workaday oppression into the air. In the little cabana I changed into my swimsuit, then stood on one end of the pool and dove. It was four o'clock on a Thursday afternoon. Down, down into the clear water I plummeted, down to where there was no time, no world! The cool water baptized me into a new, free life.

Part Four: Loose Wires

1.

A few of my friends who, like me, were back in town for the summer, had rented an apartment in a gritty neighborhood just inside the St. Louis city limits. Once in a while we played cards there. Sometimes we just hung out and read. The idea was to have a place for that, and someplace private to bring a date.

After the debacle with my father, though, I didn't feel I could live in the same house with him, and I moved into the apartment. My friends tolerated this. If they were irritated by my stretching the sense of our understanding, they never said anything. They still came by whenever they wanted.

I would stop by the house on Waterman now and then to visit Mother, trying to time those visits so that Dad would never be there. Once, though, I miscalculated. His station wagon drove up as I was leaving. He got out and climbed the hill that sloped up from the sidewalk like a chieftain approaching a rebellious contender. I was an interloper, a trespasser. The primal father began his effort to re-claim his turf.

"Get out!" he shouted.

"I'm visiting Mother! I have a right to! What are you doing here now?"

"Go get a job and take care of yourself!"

We continued our brouhaha, there on the flat hilltop lawn. We fought with words and body posture, over inches and feet, the way whole armies had during World War I. There were no blows, but Dad's words were fueled by a burning coal of a heart, and I replied with my own rage. I soon realized, however, with the sane part of my mind, that no good could possibly come of our clash. I spoke past my father to give Mother, now standing at the open front door, my parting regards, and walked down the hill to my car.

2.

Elise and I continued our evening rendezvous. Sometimes we'd go out, but more often I'd go over to her place. We'd sit in the living room, watch TV and talk with her mother. After a while her mom would go to bed. We would then retire to a den at the front of the house and indulge in kissing and foreplay that became wonderfully intense. I would leave around midnight, feeling like a king.

One night in particular, I remember striding down the walkway back to my car as a breeze blew through the branches of the huge, leafy maples that lined the sidewalk. I felt as if I owned the street, owned the night. There was no one to diminish my joy. At 20, I had a beautiful girlfriend *and* I might also be a poet!

As I got in my car and turned the key, the radio was playing "Just Call Me Angel of the Morning," a somewhat popular song that seemed as if it had been written in paradise. And I drove home, along avenues of quiet joy, of that paradise.

3.

My memories of the summer flit by like sights outside a car window, probably because quite a few of them took place in cars. There had been my first outing with Elise and her parents, to their land on the lake with their little portable "housie" on it, a couple of hours from the city. I didn't feel completely at ease with my girlfriend's parents; what young man does? But I was touched that they had invited me, and I wanted to make a good impression, and I think the day went well.

Not long after, Elise asked if I wanted to drive (she didn't drive) us to Madison to visit her sister, who was studying there for the summer. I phoned a friend in Evanston and we made a little vacation of it, staying a night in each university town and another in a motel on the way back. Her golden hair splayed on the pillow each night, and the lush patchwork fields of Illinois and southern Wisconsin passing by as she sat beside me, were like a picturesque quilt of heady waking dreams by day. Even my dad, with whom I was now somewhat reconciled, sounded envious. I wanted to spend my whole life like I was spending this summer: loving, travelling, writing.

And who was to say I could not?

4.

Underlying everything between Elise and me, somehow, was the subject of sex. If that had ever been a question with my Northwestern girlfriend, her raw passion had quickly answered it. Interesting, how relationships differed. Elise and I were affectionate companions and neither of us was a cold fish, but the matter of whether, and when, we would have sexual intercourse *loomed* over us. As we became more and more involved, it lingered behind everything we did. On our trip, we shared a bed and played, but stopped short of "the big one."

What were we, really? Serious partners? It seemed that way to me. Our connection had restored my life. I felt grateful. The idea that we would ever look back on our relationship as a "summer idyll" was ludicrous.

One day Elise invited me to go *back* to the lake, just the two of us. We set out on Sunday, packing a few things and leaving mid-morning. Arriving around noon, we spread a blanket near the shore. We dawdled, read and hiked awhile before getting out the picnic basket and having lunch. After a rest, we went for a swim. I held her in the water. Glancing over towards the nearby shore, my eyes happened to wander to one of those "jellied" strings of frog eggs, partly floating in the water and partly hanging on a thin reed.

We got out of the water and lay on the blanket in the warm late-afternoon sun.

"I think this would be a good time to make love," Elise said.

I lay looking up at the sun, shading my eyes. Nothing came out of my mouth.

"Did you hear me?" she asked

"Yes," I said. "I just don't know if I can do it right now." I turned over and embraced her. She was unresponsive.

"I'm sorry," I said. "I don't know what's wrong."

A little while later, we packed our things and drove silently back to the city. Again we passed through St. Ann, and I felt the nausea come up in my belly.

The next evening she didn't phone. I felt too vulnerable to call her. In some ways, she had been "the man" in our relationship, the one who usually initiated contact.

I tried to deal with all the loose ends that were shaking around inside me again. I really didn't know why I hadn't been able to respond, beside the lake. Did I need the security of a room, a bed? I hadn't been able to muster myself for one of the tests life was always arranging, sometimes without warning, and it'd had this night-and-day effect. Once more now, the hunger of my heart was like a lion prowling inside me, devouring me.

5.

The Director of Admissions of a small, experimental college in Florida happened to be in St. Louis soon after I'd inquired about the school. We had lunch together, talking as we ate. When we'd finished, he pronounced me admitted.

A few weeks earlier, a man from Kansas City had phoned about purchasing the Apartment Guide business. In this case, a couple of dinners and some conversation ended in his handing Dad and me a check which, while falling short of making us rich, was reasonable compensation. Dad had accepted that the Guide wasn't going to happen anymore, and had become ready to let it go. He continued to rail for years after, however, about my "hippie philosophy." He quoted words he said I'd uttered, practically up until the time of his death three decades later: "You don't believe in work! 'You do as much as you have to, to get by.' That's your philosophy." I may have said those words. I don't remember. If they'd ever been my credo, however, they've long ceased to be. The truth is far more complicated.

6.

Yet another poem came to me in a semi-trance one day, even in the midst of my turmoil over Elise's disappearance. I became mesmerized while contemplating the beauty of a peach tree whose round, colorful fruit was nearing ripeness. It seemed to represent a wholeness that is the culmination of all ripening processes in the world, a perfection pervading existence.

Across the globe that very day, Russian tanks were rolling into Czechoslovakia to put an abrupt end to what everyone had called the Prague Spring—the recent, localized thaw in the Cold War. My poem made reference to this event, ending with the lines, "On streets of Prague today / you bear your smooth fruit," implying that universal ripening prevails even over catastrophe. Through poetry, I was learning, it becomes possible to participate in the life of the entire planet!

7.

Elise continued to remain aloof. I never did call her. The loose ends inside me remained unresolved.

Finally, I couldn't take it anymore. On a whim in mid-August, I flew to Texas and spent 10 days baking in the mesquite hill country near Kerrville, where my Northwestern apartment-mate's family owned a ranch that in the summer became a camp for kids. On the way there, I stayed overnight in Austin with Herman, a young man with a huge, disheveled White-Afro and a terrible scar on his chin.

I met Herman on the street. We walked the town for hours as twilight, and then night, came on. I enjoyed Austin's Spanish, subtropical atmosphere. Herman said he'd been in Vietnam, chewing on a Pongee-stick pipe, when a bomb had gone off nearby. The impact had knocked him down and the sharp stick had gone all the way through his face.

Around 10 pm, he said he was going home, and invited me to crash at his place. It turned out that meant sleeping beside him on the double bed in his messy, clothing-strewn room.

In the middle of the night a beautiful girl came in through the bedroom door. She climbed into the bed on Herman's side, across from me, and began making love with him. I feigned sleep, but this was a bit much for me. When they finished and seemed to be sleeping themselves, I rose, picked up my duffel bag, and left as quietly as I could.

"There are many, many ways / for the terribly free / to scar their faces," I wrote my notebook on a bench a little later, about a person whose life had taken him beyond anything I could imagine.

For the flight home, after my time at the ranch, I decided to fly out of Dallas instead of Austin. That gave me a chance to thumb the couple of hundred extra miles, and possibly have more adventures. I spent an hour between rides in a cottonwood grove next to a stream that seemed to be the end of nowhere. A pick-up truck stopped and let me off two hours later by a big traffic circle outside of Tyler. It had gotten dark. Unsuccessful in getting a ride from there, I lay down in a ditch to try to sleep. After a while, huge hives broke out all over my body. Scratching myself furiously for an hour or two, I finally gave up and walked to a motel across the way and took a long, hot shower in the safe environment my room. The hives disappeared as if they'd never existed, and I slept like a baby, feeling I'd been through heaven and hell in a single night.

8.
All too soon I was back in St. Louis, getting ready to leave again, this time for Florida. My recent escapades on the road had seemed to bring experiences exponentially faster than settled life, and I felt hungry for more. I was like the blind man feeling the elephant, only this "beast" seemingly had *infinite* different kinds of features.

Underneath all this, I was still crying for my summer love. I believed I knew why Elise had dumped me, but I simply could not bear to phone her or stop by and hear it from *her*. I decided I would just start over at my new school. I'd always wanted to live in Florida.

I made my flight, heart still raw, wondering how long it would take for its scars to heal—yet even now, ready to give living another try.

Coming Into It

1.

On a Saturday morning in late September, Martin got on his bicycle and rode, under the warming Florida sun, to the bookstore of Erehwon College. Locking the bike in front of the store, he looked up to see Richard, a fellow transfer student with a full beard whom he'd once met briefly, walking towards the front door. Richard suddenly seemed to represent an unknown, alien world, and a nameless, reasonless fear arose in Martin's gut.

Martin had only been at Erehwon a couple of weeks. It was surprising to feel the anxiety surfacing already.

His first two years at Northwestern had left him feeling lost. Beyond the perimeter of his parents' dotage during his upbringing, he'd gradually discovered he couldn't control his world. As time went by, he'd become less and less able to function.

He'd transferred to Erehwon to make a new start. That idea now began to appear naïve. Richard, the store, the surrounding world and sky all seemed fuzzy. Martin felt a strong urge to get back on his bike, ride home, and hide in bed.

True, in this year of 1968, there were a lot of reasons why anyone might want to hide. The country, the whole world, in fact, seemed to be lurching towards the edge of some cliff. Riots, assassinations, and general divisiveness over Vietnam continually upped the general anxiety level. The only sanity available was whatever refuge one's own mind could provide. Martin's refuge was diminishing.

He'd felt enthused, leaving home for the first time two years before, still thinking of himself as the powerful figure he'd been as a senior in high school. He'd even had the confidence to ask girls for dates during Orientation Week at Northwestern. But when one of them responded to an attempt he made at humor while dancing with her—he didn't even remember the joke—with an abrupt, angry "You're crazy!" he'd begun to withdraw. Joining a fraternity after Rush Week, he never really felt comfortable with the brothers, and quit after two quarters. Much of his memory of the first year consisted of anonymous trudging to classes during the Chicago winter with its foot-deep snows, scarcely speaking to anyone.

In the spring, Martin became involved in a flurry of political activity on campus. A new sense of identity as a radical boosted his spirits, and the rush of energy carried him on into sophomore year. But that second winter, the lover with whom he'd lost his virginity and spent fall quarter cocooning in his room, had suddenly ended their relationship. After that, a political identity was no consolation. Martin finished the school year in a prolonged existential stupor. In June, walking away from the off-campus apartment he'd shared with one of the radical leaders, he looked back at the building and made a vow never to return to Northwestern.

Back in St. Louis for the summer, he soon noticed that this decision to start over began to put the whole Northwestern experience behind him. Creating that mental boundary brightened his mood. He'd learned of Erehwon College, an experimental school on Florida's Gulf Coast, from a high school acquaintance who was going there, and had been accepted as a transfer student after lunch with the dean of students, who happened to be visiting the Midwest. Flying to Florida after a summer with parents and friends, he'd felt confident again about the future.

The terror he felt now at the bookstore seemed far out of proportion to anything that simple shyness would manifest. Martin sensed something wrong inside, way down in a place he couldn't even see.

Perhaps something he didn't remember had happened during childhood. The class he was taking on Freud naturally led to such speculation. Regardless of the cause, though, he realized he needed to take the situation in hand—open himself up.

Right there, in front of the bookstore, Martin made a vow. Either he would go to a psychotherapist, or he would take LSD—whichever opportunity came along first.

The psychedelic drug was gaining a reputation among its adherents for its capacity to usher them to previously inaccessible depths. Martin had read Aldous Huxley's book *The Doors of Perception* and Alan Watts' *The Joyous Cosmology*, as well as several articles in popular magazines. Although he found many of the aesthetic and mystical perceptions of Huxley and Watts incomprehensible, it was clear that the psychedelic experience had opened up a new world for each of them.

As for therapy, his father had been concerned about him the summer before, and had sent him to an old army pal who'd become a psychiatrist after the war. But that had been for a single interview and an evaluation.

His mother had spoken to him once during childhood about a boy at school who "came from a broken home" and visited an analyst regularly. That little boy's mom had told Martin's that at his sessions, her son played Fish with the doctor. Martin had felt a tender caring in his mother's voice, but also a deep pity. Her words, as well as other, unspoken values in the family, had stigmatized all forms of counseling. "Not needing therapy" had long been one of the things that enabled his family to feel superior to "troubled families"—perhaps a myth they'd had to preserve for their own survival. Now it was necessary to re-evaluate this old taboo.

2.

The next day, still feeling unsettled, Martin boarded a bus on campus and rode, along with two dozen other students, to a New Party political rally in a park adjacent to a marina near downtown Sarasota. The New Party was one of several fledgling, left-liberal organizations that had sprung up after the defeat of the Democrats in the 1968 presidential election. A girl named Amy, intriguing in a tight cerulean blue dress with a gold strip at the hem that made her look like a comic book heroine, greeted him as he got on the bus. A hand of fear restrained him from sitting next to her, and after returning her greeting, he slipped into an empty row near the back.

In the park the day was sunny and comfortable, cooled by ocean breezes. The Gulf was blue and the trees and grass were lovely, bright shades of green. The world shone and sparkled, but Martin continued to feel cut off. He left the group and walked around the park alone as the amplifiers began to blare out the speaker's words. Halfway around, he came upon a mustachioed young hippie in a tall hat, a buckskin jacket, and striped bell-bottoms, standing beside a pair of arching palm trees.

"Just back from the West Coast!" he murmured from his throat. *"Got some Blue Cheer, 100 per cent pure! It's far out!"*

"How are things out west?" Martin asked, trying to sound casual. He'd taped photos of the Summer of Love on the wall above the bed of his freshman dorm room, along with a sign saying SAN FRANCISCO OR BUST, but was yet to get there.

"Far out!" the hippie said.

"How much is the acid?"

"Five bucks a tab," said the young man. "Two tabs for nine, five for twenty."

"I'll just take one," said Martin, pulling his wallet uncertainly from his pocket and getting out a five-dollar bill. The hippie took the bill, then reached into his jacket pocket, got out a tiny cellophane bag, and slipped it furtively into Martin's hand. Martin kept walking. After a hundred feet, he unclasped his fist and looked at the bag that lay in his palm. The oblong, oval pill was a pleasing robin's-egg blue, speckled with tiny green dots. He pulled out his wallet again and pushed the bag deep down behind his driver's license and Social Security card. Then he walked the rest of the way around the park, winding up back at the rally, whose main speaker had just ended his talk. People were starting to approach the snack table and then gather in little groups for conversation. Martin got a cup of coffee and listened to a campus political leader rant about how the New Party was a liberal sell-out, until it was time to board the bus back to school.

3.

A week later, having nothing to do on Saturday night, Martin was walking aimlessly around campus and ran into Tyrone, an Afro-haired Caucasian whose obsession was his electric guitar. Martin's and Tyrone's parents had befriended each other during Parents' Week, and the families had lunched together.

"What're you up to?" Tyrone, who rarely said anything, asked.

"Nothing at all," said Martin.

"Wanna drop some acid?"

"Uh…sure," Martin replied. "I just bought my first tab last week. It's right here in my wallet. Never knew if I'd ever take it at all. I guess now's as good a time as any."

"Let's go in my room," said Tyrone, motioning his head. In the bathroom, his hand disappeared into the medicine cabinet and came out holding a round, bright yellow pill. He filled a glass with water for each of them. Martin pulled the staple off his little bag, fished out the blue tablet, put it in his mouth, and washed it down.

"What do we do now?" he asked, taking a deep breath, knowing better than to ask "How do you know when you're high?"—a question he'd inquired of the long-haired, bearded friend who'd first turned him on to marijuana, spring of freshman year at Northwestern. Shortly afterward, he'd looked again and seen not his friend but the Devil, making a repeat of the question clearly unnecessary.

So now, LSD ingested, he and Tyrone went back outside and started walking the nighttime campus once more. Martin was pretty sure that something would happen, even though it seemed logically preposterous that such *tiny* pills could do very much.

After a while, he felt a kind of electricity coursing through his body, and the sky seemed electric. He looked for lightning and was surprised to see that the night was still clear.

Now the palm trees seemed to be joking with them. "The trees are holding their arms out like butlers!" he announced to Tyrone. "Maybe we should order a drink from them." Tyrone bobbed his head knowingly as he laughed. His silent laugh was static electricity and his hair looked as if he'd stuck his finger in a socket.

Martin realized he'd never get a regular conversation out of Tyrone, just these looks and nods and head-bobbing laughs. Was Tyrone really some kind of mechanical man? His last name, in fact, was *Watt*. Maybe he was just some kind of electricity terminal. It was too weird. When they came to an intersecting walkway, Martin turned onto it without a word and continued on alone, hoping Tyrone wouldn't notice—or if he did, would understand.

Everything was very funny on LSD. LSD was *about* how funny everything was! The bricks had stacked themselves up like houses of cards. The steps were walking up and down themselves, over and over. The tiles of the walkways and courtyard were a vast checkerboard where a thousand pieces might play, and the students were the pieces.

Someone came sauntering along in the shadows from the opposite direction. It was his apartment mate, Rick Shea, in his thick brown glasses, wearing a peach-colored shirt, shirttail hanging out over his khaki shorts.

"Rick, I dropped acid!" Martin told him. Rick had a sympathetic face. There were lines on his face that showed how he felt, whereas Tyrone's never gave a clue as to his feelings.

Rick frowned in serious concern, then buried the frown as he asked, "What's it like?" Rick had once mentioned that he and his girlfriend, Martha, had taken the drug.

"Well, it's all electricity! Everything's about electricity. It's crackling in everything! Tyrone's laughter sounded like an electric guitar! Everything's just pulsing, all through me, around and around. And I saw the steps marching up themselves, and how a thousand checkers could play on the tiles of the palm court. It's all so *funny*!" Martin felt his face straining as he smiled.

Rick looked at him, seriously and sadly, eyes intent across his thick glasses.

"You're way up in your head, Marty," he said. "That's *fear* you're feeling, and you don't even know it."

"Oh, my God, you're right!" Martin gasped, realizing suddenly, with horror, that unbeknownst to him, his consciousness really was stuck in a narrow box of fear.

"What are you afraid of?" Rick asked. "What is it you really want to do?"

"I want to go see Heidi," Martin confessed. Heidi was a small, cute, funny girl who wore bright-colored T-shirts over loose jeans. Martin only knew her a little, but whenever he saw her, he wanted to gather her up into his arms.

Rick smiled.

"Thank you!" Martin said and hugged him hard. Rick hugged back and then continued on his way.

4.

What time has it gotten to be? Martin wondered. Time was an immeasurable ocean. Not wearing a watch, he had no idea how much of it had passed since he and Tyrone had taken their LSD.

Heidi lived down on the Key, a mile and a half away, in a little house she rented with some friends. Martin had helped deliver a sofa there two weeks before. Now he rode his bicycle through the dark streets towards the causeway. There were only a few cars left on the Tamiami Trail. That meant it was probably late.

He still had to be careful, wearing dark clothes and all. He rode on the sidewalk when he could. The streetlights were far apart, and there could be a minute or more of darkness between pairs of headlights.

Passing a pagoda-like Chinese restaurant south of campus, Martin was no longer a mass of nerves trying to hold in the electrical energy that powered him and the universe. He'd made the turn towards what he wanted. He had faced himself, and as he'd done so, the mask of what he now realized had been a terrible superficiality had fallen away. He was Odysseus, ancient, timeless warrior, traversing the ocean of darkness between himself and his beloved Penelope—a mythic figure as ancient and strong as Orion in the sky. This LSD truly plunged you into fathomless depths that lay present, wherever you were, buried just beneath your fear and denial. People called it a drug, but that was a misnomer. Lies and advertising had drugged everyone into a walking stupor. LSD took away the blinders that hid the true significance of life.

Martin continued to ride his old, bent-up bike, but it may as well have been a Viking ship, plying unknown waters to the edge of the Earth. It seemed a long way to the house near the cul-de-sac of its quiet street a few blocks from the bay, but after a timeless interval, he arrived. Nothing seemed to be happening on the street, but light glowed from a window in the house. The light was in the front of the house. Heidi lived in a room with its own entrance to the driveway, near the back. The window there was dark.

Martin, having come all this distance, knew that again he must face and overcome his fear. He set the kickstand on the bike, walked up the driveway to her door, and knocked. There was no answer, so he knocked a little harder. Finally, he heard a shuffling inside then a click. Light came flooding under the door. It opened before him. Heidi stood there in her bathrobe, eyes half open, yawning.

"Oh. Martin," she said, looking a little puzzled.

"I dropped acid!" Martin said. Just mentioning ingesting the substance identified one as a contemporary explorer-knight. "Will you come out and talk to me? Please?"

"Hold on a minute," she said, with neither enthusiasm nor disdain that he could detect. She went back in and pushed the door closed without latching it. A moment later it started opening again, as if of its own accord. Martin looked down to see a white paw pulling it. Then a large, droopy-eared basset hound came sauntering out and looked up at him.

"Hi," Martin said, scratching him behind his ears. "What's your name?"

"His name is Jeeves," Heidi said, following her dog out. She was wearing a red T-shirt, jeans, and sandals now. The three of them walked out to the curb.

"I came all the way from campus. I was with Tyrone there, and I was uptight but didn't realize it, but then I saw Rick. Good old Rick," he went on. "He's a saint." Heidi was close friends with Martha. "He told me what I was feeling was fear, and I realized he was right, and that what I really wanted to do was come and see you."

Heidi sighed.

"I like you," said Martin, looking into her eyes, then looking down again, and catching Jeeves looking up at *him* with big, understanding, doggy eyes. He scratched the animal again, thankful to have something to do with his hands. Heidi put her hands to her forehead for a moment as if in thought, then settled them in her lap.

"I just got finished with a relationship," she said, "and I'm trying to keep things really simple for a while. I have a thesis to write, too, and…well, let's be friends, OK? I'm afraid that's about all I can offer you right now. Now I need to get back to sleep. It's 4 a.m." She rose and Martin rose, and she gave him a kiss on the cheek before walking back up to her room with her dog.

"Good night!" Martin shouted loudly from the curb as she was about to close the door.

"Ssssshhhh!" she said, putting a finger to her mouth before disappearing inside. But he was in ecstasy now. Restraint was the farthest thing from his cart-wheeling mind. Where her lips had touched his face, a garden had blossomed—a rose garden, every atom fresh and fragrant! He was living at the center of the psyche's eternal fairy tale, cast in the role of hero. Face your fear and everything blooms! Again it had happened. It was the one message life had to teach, the one action that opened all doors.

Martin knew without a doubt that later she would come to him, to his bed. Her kiss had told him. Now he need only wait. Inwardly, the eternal lovers were already reunited. All that remained was the external consummation.

The sky was losing its black, and as he rode on his bike it lightened more, as if his pedaling was *making* it light. He rode faster and faster, making the sky lighter and lighter!

He decided to pedal to the beach to celebrate this new love before going home. Heroic lines of verse began to course through his head as he sighted the expanse of the Gulf and rode towards the waves that dashed in all their exuberance upon the shore: *"And I took all I had done and gave it all to the Sea! And the Sea said, 'It is good!'"*

Martin parked and locked the bike and walked across the beach, golden in the pink dawn. Bening down, he washed his face in the effervescent salty brine. All the grime of his 20 years began dissolving and washing off in the sparkling, foaming waters. He yanked his shirt high up over his head, waved it around and around, and flung it as far as he could. Then he dashed into the ocean in his shorts, drenching them. He kept running, playing tag with Nature, colliding with the eager waves, meeting Neptune in the gentle trailers of his seaweed beard.

And then the sun, a freshly cracked egg, appeared over the horizon. Martin accepted the blessings it showered, that he could almost see, and bowed to return something to this young but mighty benefactor. As it rose higher, becoming a small, yellow pellet radiating still more happiness, he walked back to his bike, unlocked it, and rode alongside the elemental sea towards home—the First Man on the First Day of Creation.

Turning inland, he soon realized that he was completely spent from his trip and its labors and joys. In a last effort, he pedaled the mile up the trail, parking the bike in front of the apartment. Before climbing into bed, he placed an arrangement of flowers and seashells he'd gathered on the walk in front of the front door, for her to see when she came. He fell asleep wondering whether he would wake before she arrived, or whether she would let herself in and climb in beside him and shake him gently to arouse him—or possibly, do it with a kiss.

But of course, she didn't come. Not that day or the next, or the one after that. When he finally saw her one day walking on campus, she didn't run over to him and throw her arms around him. He felt completely raw and naked, but she seemed not to even notice him.

Gradually, it became clear to Martin that he'd imagined his entire scenario. His mind grew ever more raw, more naked in its pain, day by day. He struggled to hold together two worlds that were slipping away from each other—his imagined, desired one, and this deaf, brutishly solid world that didn't hear his dreams and just lumbered on and on.

He sought out a campus counselor, the sympathetic wife of a biology professor. She listened attentively, nodded, and seemed to understand. But Martin received little relief from her commiseration, and continued to vibrate with the reverberations of the shock of his waking nightmare. The worst was his total confusion about what his visions had meant. The gates of Heaven had closed and locked him out. There was certainly no way he could approach Heidi about his state, for now he clearly remembered her words: "…that's all I can offer now."

The world was solidifying again. He was powerless to stop it. His mind scanned for possible solutions to his dilemma, and came up with only one. He began to look, and listen, for a way to get hold of some more LSD.

Fare To Malcolm Bliss

Martin was driving east in his taxi down Delmar Boulevard, just inside the city limits. Blocks of dark tenements and closed shops went by in shadow. He felt a little twinge of fear, passing the lighted liquor store at Hamilton Avenue, where the African-American men stood alone or in small groups, holding brown paper bags or drinking from open beer cans. Even tonight in the cold rain they were there, standing under the eaves of the roof to keep dry.

Martin looked at the serenely smiling photo of Meher Baba, his spiritual guide, on the card he'd propped up near the center of the dashboard and felt the anxiety lift. The whole world was an illusion, and he did not have to worry about it. The picture was the one from Baba's later years, when his moustache and nose were both enormous and his whole face seemed to beam "Don't worry—be happy," which, in fact, was the caption below the picture. Some years later, an artist named Bobby McFerrin would see the card and use the words as the basis for a popular song.

There hadn't been many fares this evening. Martin was more or less passing time as he drove, listening to a jazz station playing a leisurely rendition of "All the Things You Are." The music was punctuated by occasional bursts of static followed by the dispatcher's voice calling a stand number. None of the stands were anywhere near, so Martin decided to head downtown, where business might be better.

From the day six months back when his friend Tom had suggested they get a taxi to drive, one of them working days and the other nights, the job had been an adventure, the kind of thing you'd do for the joy and experience whether you got paid or not. From the first day, he knew it would be like that. An African-American driver named Pete had taken him out for training. They'd waited at a cab stand in North St. Louis and then picked up a passenger a few blocks away, in what Martin had been trained to think of as "the ghetto". He was surprised, turning off Goodfellow Avenue onto a circular private drive of old mansions with a park in the center. He'd never known such things existed in that part of the city.

From that day on he was aware that this, rather than his years in the vast lecture halls of a university, was his education. Whether he was carrying an elderly black lady to the supermarket and back, driving a young man to visit the orphanage where he'd been raised, or, as had happened on his very first fare, discovering that the three Chinese men in the back seat were unable to tell him where they were going because they spoke no English—each shift brought surprises. The daily encounters with men, women and children of all walks of life were finally curing his insular upbringing in a suburb inhabited mostly by Jewish families like his own.

Driving along Interstate 70 at night, when the factory smokestacks were belching white smoke, Martin always imagined them to be dynamos sending the city's prayers up to God. He felt fortunate to be one of the angels ferrying people to their destinations in the vast human beehive of an American city in the late 20th century.

Approaching Union Boulevard, he put on the turn signal and got into the right-hand lane in order to cut over to Lindell Boulevard, with its long immaculate row of mansions at the edge of Forest Park. From there he'd turn east again and drive past the Chase Hotel.

The traffic light cast its red glow upon puddles disturbed by the rain. Martin stopped the cab and prepared to make the turn. A couple of hundred feet down Union, he noticed a figure waving an arm in the air. Someone appeared to be trying to flag him down.

Fare To Malcolm Bliss

The Checker cab company had a rule against picking up flaggers, but business was so bad at the moment that the prospect was tempting. This section of Union was somewhat gentrified, and Martin was not as on guard as he would have been a few blocks north. Furthermore, there was a human being out there getting soaked.

Making the turn, he eased the 200 feet forward and pressed his foot lightly again on the brake so that the sedan, with its bright gold checkerboard logo overlaid upon its green body, would stop without a skid. A tall, youngish man with a scruffy wet mop of red hair stood in the center of the street on the passenger side. He wore an old grey raincoat and his face looked pinched and haggard. As he reached for the cab door, which was still locked, Martin pushed the button on the center console to lower the passenger-side window.

"Where you trying to get?" he shouted over the rain, which was falling harder now.

"Malcolm Bliss Hospital!" shouted the young man, an Appalachian twang in his voice.

Martin considered the options. "Oh, heck, get on in," he replied after a moment. "I'm not supposed to pick up flaggers, but it's such a nasty night and the bus could be hours!" He pressed the button that unlocked the door and the young man opened it and climbed in. Martin pushed down the flag that started the fare box going, and then stepped on the gas. The rider's destination was the psychiatric building of the ancient, dilapidated city hospital that serviced St. Louis' poor. It was five or six miles away on the city's southeast side. Martin, who had long enjoyed the irony of the institution's name, had occasionally joked to friends about becoming a rock singer and using "Malcolm Bliss" as his stage name.

"How come you're going *there*?" he asked the passenger. Once people got in his cab, they became almost like family.

"Pick up my meds," the young man said matter-of-factly. Martin turned and looked at him and felt he understood more about the drawn seriousness of the fellow's face.

"I used to take psychiatric meds," Martin volunteered as he pulled back into traffic, bringing his eyes again to the windshield. He could feel the passenger's eyes on him, as if to say, *"Why is he telling me this?"*

"I had a total breakdown after some bad acid trips," he went on. "My folks sent me to a shrink. He told me I had a chemical imbalance—that I hadn't just blown my brain forever, the way I thought I had. He said there were pills that could actually re-balance me. I took them and suddenly one morning I woke up with the energy to go out and be with people again."

"Hold on a minute," said the passenger. "You said you *used* to take the pills. Doc told me I'll be takin' 'em all my life! How'd you get off?"

"It's a long story," said Martin, sighing. "First of all, I believe now that it's our consciousness that causes our chemistry—*not* the other way around! As far as getting off the pills, you see, even though they gave me energy, I never really felt quite *myself* on them. A month or two after they kicked in, I got involved with a lady and I came to feel I was cheating her, not giving her all of me, somehow. A few months passed and I just quit the pills, cold turkey. Unfortunately, I went right back to my black hole hell within a couple of weeks."

"Why'd you expect anything different?" the passenger asked.

"Oh, there's a lot I didn't tell you," Martin said. "You see, after about a month with the pills' energy, I had a *real* spiritual experience. It involved the man whose picture's on the dashboard. This *love* suddenly just wafted out of a poster of him that I saw! It included everyone and everything—it *was* everyone and everything! I knew without being told that this was God. After that, since God was in my life, I figured He'd take care of me and I wouldn't need the pills."

"But you said that you went back into the black hole."

"I did. Shows how little I knew!" Martin laughed. "Apparently, God doesn't make everything a picnic, the way I thought He would. I even tried going *back* on the pills later, and this time they didn't work! Lost the girl, too! After the most miserable year and a half you can imagine, going to a day hospital with dead-end mental patients, I finally came through to a state of genuine peace, pill free."

Martin believed in *encountering* a passenger, when he felt there was a chance to make a connection. He smiled to himself, remembering what had happened last week. He'd driven two Pentecostal ministers, in town for a convention, from the airport to their hotel downtown. He'd questioned them about the sect's practice of talking in tongues. One of them had replied, "Tongues are a gift of the Holy Spirit, but are not sufficient unless also accompanied by good works." Satisfied with that answer, Martin had felt a sudden urge to open the New Testament he'd been reading for the first time while waiting for taxi passengers. He uncannily flipped the book right to Acts 2:1, the main verse on talking in tongues.

"Son, I think you're on the right track!" the minister had remarked with a smile. It was like that. It seemed that in the cab, anything at all could happen. Another time a lady had asked Martin, "Would you let me anoint you?" Upon his consent, she applied a small amount of thick liquid to his forehead. "Thou hast anointed my head with oil," the line from the 23rd psalm, rolled through his mind. He felt deeply moved.

Martin's ecumenical mission went even beyond trying to focus on the Oneness of all religions at their core. Meher Baba said all *beings* were one—not just all religions. Martin wanted his taxi to be a travelling Sanctuary in the St. Louis night.

He and his passenger rode on in silence. Martin had decided to turn south on Kings Highway, rather than take the wet-slick expressway all the way downtown.

"Well, who *is* the guy in the picture?" the passenger asked. "He don't look like no God to me. Look at that big nose!"

Martin smiled. "That's what my dad says. His name is Meher Baba. He lived in India from 1894 until 1969. If you saw a picture from when he was younger, you might say he was the handsomest man who ever lived. But whatever he looked like, he said his body was only a coat."

"Does he have a church?" the passenger asked.

"He didn't come to start a church," Martin said. "He said he was the Avatar, the same one who came to Earth as Jesus 2000 years ago, as Zoroaster, Ram, Krishna and Buddha before that and later as Mohammed. He said he comes back whenever we humans begin to forget why we're here. The Avatar never comes to start a religion; his followers do it later. Baba was also silent in this Advent. He didn't speak for the last 44 years of his life. He communicated in gestures and on an alphabet board, and said that when he breaks his silence, it will raise human consciousness to a new level."

"If there ain't no church, what you do you do for fellowship?" the young man asked. "You got to have fellowship, don't you?" Martin was surprised at how his passenger, in spite of his rough grammar, seemed to grasp everything he had heard.

"I used to live in Berkeley, California, and I went to Baba meetings there. St. Louis doesn't have a group yet. Last year I was led to a kind of stand-in group, a mystical Christian group called the Holy Order of MANS. The *feeling* I get is the same as from Baba. It *is* Baba, actually. I even had a *vision* of Him there once! They just call Him by a different name, and I have to watch my words a little bit around some of them."

Martin's face suddenly lit up as he spoke. *"Hey!"* he exclaimed. "I just realized the Order's community meeting is going on right now, a few blocks away from here! Why don't you let me take you? I'll turn off the meter!" Martin reached over and pushed up the flag. Then he turned right, weaving through the quiet, residential streets on the southwest side of the city, near the botanical gardens. Finally, he pulled the cab into a vacant parking space alongside the little park on Thurman Avenue.

"Where we at?" asked his passenger. "I don't see no church."

"It's just a little storefront," Martin said. "It's down at the end of the block. You'll see."

"Man, I hope you're not messin' with me," the passenger said in a raised voice that sounded slightly ominous.

"I'm not," Martin reassured him.

"Well, you don't have no idea who you're talkin' to," said his guest. "I wanted to be a minister. I studied in seminary, two years! You want to know why I quit?"

"Why?"

"Because I couldn't find God! Now you're talkin' about God like He's somethin' I can just reach out and touch any time I want? Well, I don't want to hear no bullshit! You *show* me God, right now!"

"It's not quite that simple," Martin said.

"Hold it!" the passenger shouted before Martin could continue. "You're throwin' me a line of crap! I ain't gonna take it!" Suddenly, the passenger flicked his hand out and pushed the button on the center console that locked all the doors. Then he pushed another one that closed the power window on the driver's side.

Martin felt like a fly caught in a spider web. These commands and actions sounded suspiciously like a *modus operandi*. Who knew what this fellow had done before?

"You better produce, damn it!" the passenger continued. "Show me God or I'm gonna *cut* you!"

He was reaching into his pocket. There was no way to tell if he was bluffing. In a flash, Martin pulled up on the handle of his door and sprung it open. *"Jai Baba!"* he shouted automatically, bursting from the car to take advantage of what, for all he knew, was his last opportunity.

He put his head down and churned his arms as he ran, dashing two full blocks before looking back.

No one was following, at least not that he could see. He slowed to a walk, still careful to stay in the shadows, and crossed the street. Then he backtracked to the storefront, which was all dark. He had arrived too late for the meeting. His friend Michael, the storefront's caretaker, had already locked up and gone home. Fortunately, though, Michael lived next door. Circling back up the front steps of the adjoining house, Martin knocked on the door.

"Yes?" came a voice. A hand pushed aside the curtain over the little window and a face looked out.

"Michael! Quick! Open up!"

Michael, hearing the urgency in Martin's voice, quickly pulled open the door. "What happened?" he asked.

"I brought a guy here in my taxi, to come to the communion service. We were on the way to Malcolm Bliss Hospital so he could get his meds. He seemed interested in God and I thought you guys might be able to help him. But when I parked, he insisted I show him God, right then! Like I could just pull God out of a hat! He started getting hostile, and locked the car doors and shut the windows. Said he was gonna cut me! I didn't wait around to find out if he really meant it."

"Where is he now?" asked Michael.

"I don't know. The cab was parked a couple blocks back when I ran."

"Let's sneak back and take a look. We can come up from behind the trees on the other side of the street. Who knows if it'll even be there anymore?"

They circled back quietly. The cab was indeed gone. They walked back to Michael's and called the police, who soon came and began questioning Martin, filling out the stolen vehicle report.

"What kind of car was it?" one of the policemen asked.

Fare To Malcolm Bliss

"Green," said Martin. The policemen looked at one another and one of them rolled his eyes. Martin felt for a moment as if the crime was no longer a stolen vehicle, but his being a man who didn't know the difference between a Plymouth and a Chevy.

Michael drove him home. He went to bed and awoke next morning to the ringing of the phone.

"Good morning, Martin, this is Mrs. Rizzo." Mrs. Rizzo's late husband had left her the Checker company in his will. "Your taxi's been found by the police," she said. "There's no damage, and the keys were right in the ignition. You can pick it up here at the garage, and get back to work any time you want."

"That's really good news," Martin said. "Where'd they find it?"

"In the parking lot right across from Malcolm Bliss Hospital," Mrs. Rizzo replied. "Wonder what the fellow was doing over there?"

The Key Turned

Part One

1.

It was around 9:30 on a breezy night in the early spring of 1978. I parked my taxicab outside my parents' house in the St. Louis suburbs and went in the basement door to the "office" I maintained there. The old-linoleum-floored room and adjoining bathroom had been intended as a maid's quarters when the house was built around 1920. As a boy, I'd used it at different times as a playroom, a pet sanctuary, a chemistry lab, and a darkroom.

I got right down to business with my guitar and tape recorder. This particular night, a desperation I'd watched grow in my heart for a couple of weeks had become unbearable, and I knew I had to take action.

It was actually my second try at this. A bare repetition of the first attempt, however, would not be sufficient. Two months before, in the deepest cold of winter, I'd had to recognize, during another evening plying my cabbie rounds, that I had "personal feelings" for Eleanor, the pen pal and phone companion who'd gradually, over the past year, become my best friend.

You know how it is. At a certain point, you just have to ask the question and accept the answer. I'd bravely dialed her number that night, and instead of bandying about with some anecdote from my day to make her laugh, had gone straight into stammering out my admission of feelings with the best words my heart and mind could put together. Her answer had been a quick, dismissive "No." As she'd realized what I was saying, her voice had morphed from its usual friendly enthusiasm into a kind of dull, bored monotone. The initial "No" had said it all, but then she'd added, "I could never be with a man again. God is my only lover for the rest of this life."

Strangely, as she spoke those words, her voice betrayed her New York origins for the first time since I'd known her. With *that* voice, *she* was something of a turn-off, too, as a part of myself not involved in the drama wryly observed.

I'd had no plans to try and batter down her defenses. It had seemed pointless, since she'd been so adamant. I went back to my taxi job with a clear mind and a capacity to be present. Now that I'd "gotten that out of my system," I would simply see what else life had to offer.

2.

In a few weeks our active friendship, which had understandably lapsed after my call, resumed. You know how that is, too, perhaps. Eleanor and I had gotten used to one another.

We'd met at the Meher Spiritual Center in Myrtle Beach, South Carolina, two years earlier. The Center is named for Meher Baba, an Indian spiritual master, born in 1894, who remained silent for the last 44 years of his life. His name means "Merciful Father" and his devotees, myself included, believe him to have been the world messenger or Avatar of our age—as Buddha, Jesus, and Krishna each were of theirs.

After a while Eleanor and I, for different reasons, had both moved back to where our families lived. By then, though, we'd become important to one another, and kept in touch regularly. We had similar family backgrounds and a unique personal connection. Now, we'd discovered our relationship could be submerged by events like my recent confession without being permanently sunk. I was glad.

We resumed our letters and phone calls. In another couple of weeks, however, I noticed voices inside me once again singing hymns to her as I drove through the St. Louis night in my Checker-taxi "Rosinante."

And so, on this second night—*"On a dark night, kindled in love with yearnings,"* in the words of St. John of the Cross, my favorite poet at the time—I resolved to do *something* more than make a mere phone call. Not knowing what that might be, I asked Meher Baba inwardly and right away, felt an intuitive answer. Thinking they might come in handy, I'd leaned the guitar against a wall and placed my little reel-to-reel, the best thing back then for saving spoken or sung material, on the table.

I knew *lots* of sublime songs. A few "I" had written. Others I'd collected. Inspiration was so accessible during this period that I felt whatever else was needed would surely offer itself to be created on the spot. The thrill of brailing the outlines of a pattern as yet partly unknown began to quicken my spirit.

I recorded several devotional songs of my own composition, then added a beautiful, little-known Afro-American spiritual entitled "Long, Long Journey," along with Peter, Paul and Mary's "Man Come Into Egypt," and the old Shaker hymn, "Wondrous Love." I also incorporated a song each by Bob Brown, Bill Meyer and Ward Parks, three inspired songwriters devoted to Baba. Their songs manifested the presence of the Master, who had finished his work and "dropped his body" in early 1969, yet could be felt, many asserted, even more powerfully now than when he had walked the earth.

I went on to create and record a simple but melodic version of "Dark Night of the Soul," the short poem to which the author, John of the Cross, had devoted a whole book of explication. The poem had become a theme of those years. Baba had referred to the world as "this darkness which you think is light," and our path to God seemed to be a veiled one, taking place in the midst of everyday life. I wasn't sure exactly what all of that meant. Certain events, however, seemed to partake of the mystery.

Once, for example, I'd been helping my friend Sister Ann of the Holy Order of MANS in the tiny garden plot that a St. Louis Public

Library branch let her use. She'd somehow misplaced the gate key, but suddenly, I almost stepped on it. It was as though its location had been *revealed* to me, buried in some grass. Sister Ann thanked God—whom I called Baba and this dear lady knew as Jesus—for my assistance. I felt a divine beauty and mystery in our collaboration.

3.

Two hours after entering my sanctum, I held what I thought was the finished cassette tape in my hand. It contained more than half an hour of inspired, mystically-based music. But as I addressed a padded envelope to my beloved and prepared to insert the tape, I felt something was missing. Immediately, I realized what that was. There was no "personal" element to let Eleanor know how I felt about *her!*

Once more, I looked and asked within. Spring was just beginning to transform the world, and you could feel it in the night air, but a seemingly perpetual spring had been in bloom in my life for some time. This was all the more miraculous because it had arisen out of such a deep, dark winter. Baba had described the advent of the Avatar every 700 to 1400 years as the "springtide of Creation," and I felt fortunate to be alive. There seemed no limit to what was possible, so I was surprised, but not *that* surprised, when almost immediately a new song wafted up and began singing itself inside me. I grabbed my guitar, inserted the tape back into the recorder, and turned it on to record. Starting with an F chord, I began singing the chorus:

> Do you know, my friend,
> do you know?
> Do you know how much I love you,
> do you know?

The song reminded me of ballads by the popular Gordon Lightfoot. The chorus was perfect. I turned off the recorder, wrote down several verses that came to mind, and then turned the machine back on. I sang the last verse into the mic:

> My love is like an ocean,
> and wants to flow to you,
> and when it does
> I'll ride there on its waves.

Suddenly, even as I continued into the last chorus, I "saw," swirling and spreading within me, a brilliant, shimmering rainbow of light like an aurora borealis. I felt, with complete conviction, that "the key had been turned." Meher Baba had occasionally used that phrase. In most cases, he said, he did his spiritual work through ordinary means. Once in a while, however, he had to "turn the key." An Australian disciple charged with purveying Baba's message in his country had complained after years of effort that he'd done his best, but there had been almost no results. Baba had gestured, "Do not worry, I will turn the key," and, in fact, literally made a gesture of doing so. Following that, the Australian's situation had changed dramatically.

Satisfied after recording the completed song, I packaged up the tape, stamped it, and dropped it in the mailbox across the street from my parents' house. Then I went back out to my taxi and finished up the night's driving.

4.

Very soon after that night, a curious and totally unexpected chain of events began to unfold in my life. I had anticipated going on with my taxi driving indefinitely. My stated goal was to raise enough money to make a pilgrimage to Baba's tomb-shrine in India, since he had expressed a wish that each devotee make the journey at least once in his or her lifetime. It was easy to see, however, that as much as I enjoyed ferrying passengers safely through the night, I was only earning enough money to pay my expenses and have a little spending money on the side. I'd *never* get to India that way.

Around a week after my nighttime musical session and song-epiphany, my overnight taxi shift ended, as usual, at 10 a.m. I left my cab at the garage for my weekly two days off, and drove my own car straight to a nearby park to unwind. As I sat, relaxing under a tree, a sudden thought came through my head as if placed there by someone: *"If you get a job on a Mississippi River boat, you'll be in India in a month."*

The statement was true, I realized. Why hadn't I thought of it before? I'd lived for a month on a towboat pushing barges several summers earlier during college, and had earned $1750. With room and board provided, I'd saved nearly all of it. Round-trip tickets to India were around $850.

I drove straight to the National Maritime Union and renewed my membership. I sat down in one of the rows of chairs, opened a book, and waited for my name to be called. Nothing happened the first day, but on the second morning, I received posting to a boat docked at Alton, Illinois, just a few miles to the north. My parents drove me up there, and I became a sailor again.

5.

A deckhand works six hours on and six hours off, 24/7. The work can be very demanding. It involves ratcheting barges together by inserting a bar into the handle of a metal device and pumping like hell. This tightens the thick cables that connect two barges. Fifteen or so barges, as you might imagine, have to be *very* tightly wired in order to ply the great river without being pulled apart.

When a tow comes through a port, it might drop off one or two of its barges and add a new one. Occasionally, the deckhands have to undo the whole tow and make up another one within a day or so. In a place like

New Orleans, where the sun often burns pitilessly overhead, working two such shifts in a day is grueling.

The part of the work I liked best was holding the end of a rope—a potentially lethal job, for I'd heard stories of men being cut in half when one broke—at the end of the tow as we'd drift into a canal lock at 3 a.m., the river unbelievably beautiful and silent in the mist. As we'd enter the lock, I'd throw the end of the rope to a man on land. He would then secure our boat and its barges to the shore until the water level had been raised or lowered enough for us to proceed.

One day, a couple of weeks into my month on the boat, we had our first mail call. My foreman handed me a thick envelope with my parents' return address scratched on it in my father's scraggly handwriting. Inside was another envelope with my beloved's name and return address. My fingers trembled as I raced to open it.

Just as I'd known would happen, Eleanor declared herself mine. "I will follow you anywhere," she wrote, in keeping with her rather dramatic nature. She added, "You are my master!" Deconstructed, this latter statement was not as radical as it sounds. I took it to mean that she saw the Master *in* me. In the East, marriage partners are taught to regard the spouse as an embodiment of God.

I walked out on deck and looked at the Mississippi. This far north in Iowa, the river appeared clean and clear. I daydreamed of what the next few weeks would bring: flying to rendezvous with her in Miami Beach, her home town; soon after that, our wedding; and finally, a triumphant trip to India for our honeymoon!

A few days later, the towboat had engine trouble in St. Paul, Minnesota, and we went into dry dock. The city rose in front of us, a golden sun reflecting off her glass skyscrapers. During my six hours off the next morning, I took a walk into town and phoned Eleanor from a booth in the Radisson Hotel. We swore our love to one another for five minutes, and talked about our plans.

As I hung up, though, the triumph in my heart was almost instantly replaced by a cold realization that I needed to confide to her certain things I hadn't yet shared. Mostly, they had to do with an emotional trauma I'd suffered at around age seven, and its effects. I had not heard the phrase "post-traumatic stress disorder" yet, but I realize now, had personified it. Many of the dragons I'd had to slay in life up to that point had been related to it. My sexuality and capacity for relationships had been affected both by the trauma itself and by the 20 years of shamed secrecy that had followed. There'd simply been no one in my life whom I'd felt I could talk to about this, until just a couple of years earlier.

From the Radisson, I walked a few blocks to an old trolley-car diner I found near the river. For some unknown reason, nearly everyone there looked as if he or she had been a photographic subject for Diane Arbus. The food was good, though. After breakfast I ordered more coffee, pulled out a notebook from my shoulder bag, and wrote out what I needed to share with Eleanor. From the diner, I trekked directly to the downtown post office and stamped and mailed my latest missive.

The next morning, the boat's engine was ready to go. We spent the morning assembling a tow to take back downriver, and departed in mid-afternoon. Throughout the next week, as I worked and rested, I nursed some mild anxiety about my beloved's reply.

It came on the next mail call. We were back in Alton, Illinois, on our way to deposit some of our barges along the Ohio River, a hundred miles or so south. This time, it was a one-sentence telegram: *"I will walk through the fires of hell with you."*

6.

The boat turned down the Ohio and then turned around again somewhere past Louisville. At Paducah, Kentucky, not too far from the river's confluence with the Mississippi, my month's stint was up. I got off the boat, had lunch, and caught a Greyhound back to St. Louis. The bus got me in late at night, but mid-morning, I went upstairs at my folks' house and called Eleanor. The afternoon light gracefully filtered through the blinds on my parents' bed, on which I sat for our lovers' conversation and planning session.

After the call, I began phoning airlines. There was no reason to stay in St. Louis for more than a day or two, now that my life would only move forward by going to be with her. Mother and Dad were a bit nonplussed by the speed of events, but they were happy that my life seemed to be filling with good things, after all I'd been through in my twenties. They drove me to the airport the next night.

The Eastern Airlines flight was one of those "pinch-yourself-to-make –sure-it's-real" intervals. Then, there she was, waiting at the gate, her curves showing under a black turtleneck and white pants, smiling at me with such love that all I could do was pick her up in my arms. After my bag came around on the carousel, she led me to her car in the parking garage, and we drove out into the decidedly tropical Florida night. We crossed the causeway to Miami Beach and turned down Collins Avenue to South Beach, the old part of town that was not yet trendy the way it is today. We pulled into the lot adjoining the Ocean Sun, the seniors' home her parents owned, where Eleanor both worked and had an apartment.

After our bodies had said what they needed to say to one another, we put on swimsuits and went across Ocean Drive to the beach. It was around 10 p.m., and tame little whitecaps were breaking under the fluttering coconut palms. God seemed to be giving me everything my heart desired. Here I was with a beautiful companion who loved me, on a tropical beach. I'd been in love with the tropics since my childhood, making Mom drive me around St. Louis looking for papayas, mangoes and coconuts, which in those days were hard to find.

During the next few days, Eleanor took me to visit her haunts and meet her friends. Her parents welcomed me. She'd told her dad I was a writer, and he was, too, it turned out. He'd written a novel and asked me if I'd read it and make suggestions. Her mom reminded me of my own mother—two ladies raised in the East Coast Jewish culture of the same era.

A week later, our friend Irwin officiated at our wedding at Miami Beach City Hall, with most of the local Baba community in attendance. After the ceremony, Eleanor and I walked between parallel lines of rice-and-confetti-throwing friends. I got in the driver's seat of her car to take us up the coast to New York City, where we'd catch our flight to India. My new wife, sitting in the passenger seat, asked me to look at her. As I did, she tied a colorful bandanna around my head. When she had it just right, I turned the ignition key and we were off.

7.

We almost didn't make it to India. A good deal more than 1,000 miles lay between us and our flight. As we drove, the energy of being together was so intense that Eleanor began to say we were "living the New Life," emulating a special phase of Meher Baba's life between 1949 and 1951, during which he had wandered about India with a small group of companions.

Perhaps, indeed, God was with us enough where we were, I began to feel. The subtext of this was that, as newlyweds, we were "cleansing one another" emotionally. In addition to lovemaking, this took the form of stopping the car occasionally to, as we began to call it, "practice dying." This had to do with consciously turning to face deep, even threatening emotions that were being stirred up by our intimacy, and remaining vulnerable as we discussed them. Sometimes, in a secluded place, we would enact a spontaneous psychodrama. I was usually the one being worked on in our relationship, with the dramatic material emerging from my "charged" subconscious. Some scenes simulated violent encounters that may or may not have actually occurred in past lives.

All I know is that the force pulling up buried emotions was almost overwhelming. I found that I carried a lot of hostility towards women, which had apparently been bottled up for quite a while. A lot had happened in my childhood that, as I've written, I could not speak of until only a year or so before I'd first met Eleanor. It still sometimes felt as if the lid had been taken off a great, boiling cauldron.

One example of the kind of surprises surfacing during this period took place even before our road trip. One evening in Miami Beach, we were sitting together on some boulders that made a kind of sea wall sloping down to Biscayne Bay. All of a sudden, for no reason I'm aware of, I became "possessed" by feelings of self-hate rising from deep inside. The feelings were so powerful and so "other" that they seemed to grab my body and propel it towards the water with great force. I believe the only reason I didn't drown was the steadying effect of Eleanor sitting nearby. Her presence gave me the forbearance to stop just shy of the plunge. Nothing remotely similar has ever happened. Though aspects of what took place during my time with Eleanor remain mysterious to me even today, my sense is that I've felt permanently lighter, emotionally, since our time together.

8.

We had a reprieve from such intensity when we reached Myrtle Beach. As a married couple, we were permitted to share a cabin at the Meher Spiritual Center. Before retiring there for the night, we rendezvoused with and received congratulations from many friends.

Back on the road, though, the energy level intensified even further. By the time we reached central North Carolina, we both realized that we were in way beyond our understanding. We agreed that we needed to stop wandering and make an immediate beeline for our flight.

In the waiting room at Kennedy airport, a thin Indian man I'd never seen before abruptly walked up to me and said, "The soul is a butterfly that is meant to land on flowers and draw nectar. But you are a butterfly who has been landing on shit!"

His words filled me with dread. Were all Indians psychic? Was what we had been doing *evil*? I felt like a bag full of "stuff" from my entire life and probably many past lives. Eleanor and I had only been trying to follow intuition—or so we'd believed. Baba had said in his *Discourses*, "Ultimate Reality…can be known fully only by *bringing the unconscious into consciousness*." I'd thought the two of us might end up as "new age healers" who could help others go through what we'd been through ourselves. Had I been deluding myself? Had we just been indulging ourselves, playing with the unconscious and its contents?

I was no longer sure of anything at all.

Part Two

1.

We disembarked from our plane, collected our bags, and emerged out into the moist air and beggar-thronged area outside the Bombay airport. Eleanor, who'd been to India twice before, hustled us into a waiting rickshaw that drove us downtown. After a restaurant snack in the hopelessly exotic and New-York-crowded center of the city, we found a taxi, larger and more comfortable than a rickshaw. Eleanor bargained with the driver about the price, while I gawked at my surroundings. Before long, we were off in one of the ubiquitous black Ambassador cars, belongings stashed in the trunk. For hours we negotiated the vast city with its numerous moss-covered high-rise residences and dozens of large and small commercial centers. Finally, we emerged onto the main road to Pune, as the highway signs said even then, before the anglicized spelling, Poona, was officially dropped.

Pune is the city of Meher Baba's birth. We were to be hosted there by Baba's brother Jal before going on to Meherabad, where Baba's tomb is, some 50 miles further on. Today there is a Mumbai-Pune expressway. While travelling along it you might sometimes swear, given the presence of such things as a neon golden arch rising high into the night sky, that you were on an American interstate. Back then, however, the only road was a one-lane, sometimes-unpaved path leading straight through numerous villages. Dogs would be sleeping in its center and know instinctively just when to get up so as to move a hair's breadth or so shy of a speeding car.

Between villages, the road wound through fields and jungle. The Western Ghats had appeared in the distance, and before long we would be climbing them. But as I peered out the window, and Eleanor wrote in her journal, we both suddenly realized that our taxi was slowing down, and in fact was about to stop, in the middle of one of the more remote jungle stretches.

"Why did we stop?" I asked the driver.

"Engine trouble."

Now we were stuck in a remote part of a country I'd been in for all of four hours.

"What are you going to do?" asked no-nonsense Eleanor. "We can't wait for long; we have someone expecting us. Can you call another car?"

Our driver did the sideways head-wag Indians do and disappeared into the bush, leaving us alone. I retrieved our bags from the trunk and piled them in front of us, in order to be ready to get in a new taxi. Promptly, it started to drizzle. That didn't seem like a big deal to me. Everything we had was secure inside a waterproof bag of some kind, or in the case of my guitar, in its vinyl case. A stringed instrument called a *bulbul* that Eleanor had brought was in a latched wooden box. My wife had followed the driver down the footpath to find out where he had gone, seeming completely comfortable in India and unafraid of dacoits, snakes, or anyone or anything else that might be lurking.

Awaiting her return, I lounged on my duffle bag, finding it rather comfortable, and let the fine drops of rain fall on my face. I had gone into a pleasant daydream when I heard a rustling in the brush. As I opened my eyes, a loud, irritated voice said, *"What are you doing?"*

It was Eleanor. It seemed obvious what I was doing, but I said, anyway, "Just relaxing."

"You left my bulbul out here in the rain?" she asked in disbelief.

"Nothing's really getting wet," I said. "These aren't even really drops; they're like pinheads of rain." As I uttered those words, it appeared as if knives came flying at me from her eyes.

"You start picking up everything and putting it back in the car, right now!" she demanded.

I was dumbfounded. Where was my beloved? I didn't know this belligerent person! I stood up and began lifting our bags, careful to secure the bulbul first. In a couple of minutes everything was back in the trunk, but just then we heard an engine. Another car, bearing a second driver, along with our first one in the passenger seat, entered the clearing and stopped.

"He will take you," said the first driver, pointing to the second. I reopened the trunk and transferred everything to the new car. We settled up with the first driver, although I had no idea how he'd contacted this new fellow. I imagined there was a village or something down the path, but as Eleanor hadn't reported on her little trek, that thought was only conjecture. We folded our hands to the first driver, who was apparently going to wait for a tow, and got into the new taxi.

"We're going to Pune, did he tell you?" Eleanor asked.

"Yes, yes," replied the driver with a head-waggle as the car began bouncing along.

Eleanor turned to me. I hoped that the newly unpleasant atmosphere would somehow go away, but her look seemed to indicate that my wish would not be granted.

"Do you like wet bulbuls or dry bulbuls?" she asked.

"What?"

"I said, do you like wet bulbuls or dry bulbuls," Eleanor repeated.

I sighed, realizing that she was making me recite a catechism.

"Dry ones," I said compliantly.

"Are you sure?"

"I'm sure," I promised her as we came into the next village. The car kept moving; the next dog got up from its sleeping spot in the road; and soon we were past this cluster of huts, too. We began climbing the ghats, both of us quiet. I don't know what Eleanor was thinking, but I was contemplating my shock. How ironic it seemed that just as we were nearing the place of all places that was our destination, our honeymoon's bucket of sweetness had sprung its first leak!

2.

Eleanor had told the driver that our hotel was near the Pune train station. She'd made our arrangements, and I was all but unaware of the specifics. Pune, which has more than quadrupled its population in the last four decades, was a mid-sized city in those days. Turning at the station, the driver wove his way to the National Hotel, a small green building surrounded by lush gardens. The *bagwallas* got our things from the trunk as we paid the driver and then walked up several steps to the lobby.

The hotel had a peaceful, secluded look. In a tall bookcase with glass doors were several books about the Bahá'í religion, apparently the faith of the owner. We signed the ledger and followed the two bellboys outside and along the corridor lined by bamboo railings that led to our room.

The room was spacious and radiated simple charm. The beds were of the Indian *charpoi* variety, with sleeping platforms of knotted rope similar to the one in Meher Baba's room in the house built for him at the Myrtle Beach Center. There was also a fireplace.

It was only when we were securely ensconced there that I began to realize how utterly exhausted I was. We had been traveling for more than 24 hours. Eleanor and I showered and put on clean clothes, and immediately afterward, we heard a knock at the door. As I turned, I saw the big end of a black, folded umbrella sticking through the door, which we'd left ajar. A moment later a small, stocky man dressed in white, with a black, Eastern-style cap on his head, entered the room and said in a loud voice, "Ah, Eleanor!" My wife was already on her way over to greet him.

"Jal!" she exclaimed, giving him the most loving embrace. They proceeded to talk, and I, sitting on the raised table that was my bed, felt my exhaustion more acutely than ever. Suddenly, it was a major task to keep my eyes open and make sure I didn't fall to the floor. My awareness was starting to dim when, a moment later, I heard Jal shout, "Ah, and you must be Martin!"

He was smiling widely and advancing toward me. "Martin!" he said jauntily. "I see Baba's Love *shining* in your eyes!" I forced myself to stand and embrace the Avatar's brother, even as I wondered, *how can he see anything besides fatigue?*

"Welcome to India, Martin!" Jal went on. "Back in America, you were like a little frog climbing the walls of the Well of Illusion. Now, you have come to India and you have *jumped*"—he made the word truly leap—"out of the well!"

"Really?" I asked, wide-eyed. Could it be that simple? *My gosh*, I thought. *What if it really is?*

"I am so happy to meet you, Martin," Jal said. I remembered the aerogramme letter that I'd received from him after completing arrangements for the trip. "Dear Loving Brother Martin," it had begun, "I was so happy to hear you are coming to India and will be able to enjoy Beloved Baba's love and bliss eternally." I'd felt this letter to be, in spirit, like the loving epistles of John or Peter in the New Testament.

Reading it had been another of those "pinch myself" moments in which I'd realized that somehow, in all my fumbling, I'd become connected with something magnificent and sublime beyond measure.

Jal said, 'Now, Eleanor, you come here, as well." As she approached, he continued. "Get a good night's sleep, both of you, and be ready for breakfast at 8 a.m. I will meet you at the hotel restaurant. After breakfast, we'll go and see some of Baba's places here in Pune. Now let us embrace once more." We each embraced him, and this messenger of joy went back out into the chirring darkness, while Eleanor and I got ready for a well-deserved night of sleep.

3.

For the next week, we were children under the care of a loving uncle. Jal met us every morning at the National Hotel restaurant where, by the way, the British-style breakfasts were delicious. He regaled us with stories of his brother, the Avatar; told us jokes; embarked on shaggy dog tales that often seemed to be about "a miser," and had me wondering obliquely whether he might be talking about us; and listened to any personal problems we might be having. Another American couple, the Johnsons, joined our little company as well. The five of us did almost everything together.

The first day, we went to the house where Baba and his siblings had grown up, and where Jal currently lived. Eleanor and I sat together in the room where, after his Divinity was unveiled by the kiss of an ancient Muslim woman named Hazrat Babajan in 1913, and until he began his work as a fully-realized Master some years later, Baba would sometimes sit and bang his head against the wall to try to contain his Oceanic consciousness. You could still see the blood spots here and there. Being there was a powerful experience. The room felt like a birthing ground for a new age.

Jal took us to the tomb of Babajan; to a museum commemorating the site of Guruprasad, Baba's summer home that had been torn down in 1971; to a cave Baba had frequented, also during the period after Babajan's kiss; and to the Pune zoo, where an elephant named Sumitra would trumpet every time she heard Baba's name.

He also took us on more recreational, "touristy" outings to shops and restaurants. Once, when we were at a little clothing shop, where I had no interest in the piles of bargain apparel my companions were avidly perusing, I noticed Jal sneaking off, about to go out the door. When he saw me looking, he motioned for me to follow. We crossed the street and sat down at a table at an outdoor chai shop. Jal said in a conspiratorial tone to the waiter, "Two chai." When the cups of tea arrived, he looked at me intently and very pointedly said, "Drink slow."

The similarities between the curious situation I was in and the stories I'd read in books, about Enlightenment being imparted through a cup of tea, teased my imagination. I drank slowly as instructed, and waited for something to happen. But in a moment or two Jal simply said, "Now let us go back to the others," and that ended my fantasy.

Across the street in the shop, one of those little ones with the pull-up aluminum front doors that leave the establishment open to the air, my companions still appeared to be going through clothing and seemed not to have noticed our absence. I took up my former place near the front of the store and waited for them to finish. In a moment, I noticed Jal standing on the opposite side of the shop, also near the front, leaning on his umbrella. He turned his head in my direction and, enunciating very clearly, asked me, *"Who are you?"*

This was the question Meher Baba had said is the *only* real question—that the soul "tests and discards innumerable false answers" before, after innumerable reincarnations, arriving at the real and final answer, "I am God."

Suddenly we were back in my God-realization scenario. Ah, so that's it, I reasoned! You have to *say* it before you can feel it! And with all due solemnity, I turned to Jal and gravely pronounced, *"I am God."*

Immediately he made a face, as though he'd eaten a lemon. Then he proceeded to lecture me, in no uncertain terms, *"Don't say you are God! Don't say you are a Master, don't say you are a Saint! Do not say anything about yourself. Forget yourself, and just say, 'BABA is Master. BABA is God.'"*

I listened one-pointedly, astonished at the elaborate means Baba's brother had gone to in order to convey this lesson. Not that I had really been prone to saying such things as he warned against; but it seemed that now I would be protected from them for the rest of my life!

4.

One evening Jal took us out to dinner at a very fancy restaurant called Dreamland. The tuxedoed waiters were like artists. The dinner of covered-dish items was served like a symphony. The food was delicious, and the *second* any of us finished our portion of an item, a waiter was immediately at the person's side, silently and politely offering another helping from a huge silver platter.

I marveled at the sumptuous feast as I made my way through two whole plates of delectable repast, but was suddenly struck by a realization: *wait a minute*, I thought to myself. *This place is called Dreamland! Did you come to India for more dreams? No, you came to awaken*!

The next time the waiter came by with his huge platter of additional helpings, I simply put my hand up, smiled, and said, "No, thank you." He instantly departed for another table. No one was *forcing* Illusion on me, I realized. It was simply up to *me* to say no.

5.

Eleanor and I took a bus to Ahmednagar and spent several days at Baba's abode there. I thrilled to bow down at his tomb-shrine, or *samadhi*, for the first time. There were not many visitors then, so we had ample time to sit inside the structure, as well as to hear Baba's close disciples Eruch and Mani speak in Mandali Hall about their days with Baba, and to meet Baba's beloved, Mehera J. Irani, whom he said was the purest soul in the universe.

Whereas today the Meher Pilgrim Retreat, located within a picturesque quarter-mile walk of the samadhi, caters lovingly to the simple needs of pilgrims, while managing, at the same time, to be palatial in its comfort, most visitors before 1980 stayed in hotels in town and commuted the nine miles to and from Meherabad each day. We put up at the Sablok, which was the closest thing—but not very close—to a hotel catering to Westerners. I found it an adventure. Besides, we were newlyweds, and any place where I could be with my beloved was paradise to me.

6.

Back in Pune, though, new spats began to break out between Eleanor and me. Jal had once described me as "like a little child." In character with that description, I brought our difficulties straight to "Uncle," instead of pretending that everything was okay.

The first time I did so was at the hotel. Jal pulled a rope and scissors from his pocket and asked me to cut the rope in two. When I did, he crumpled the two pieces together in his hands. A moment later, he asked me to take the rope from him and straighten it out. It was intact once more! "Just a trick," I suppose, but it really did re-harmonize us for a while.

The next time Jal gave us instead a three-word suggestion, which he delivered melodically: "Talk in song." Again, his prescription worked!

The Key Turned

Singing to one another our practical questions, our "sweet nothings," and even our disagreements, we became magically "in tune" with one another for the rest of the day and most of the next!

However, we didn't feel able to sing to each other forever, and yet another row erupted before long. A couple of days before our departure, as the five of us prepared to enter a restaurant for afternoon tea, Jal whispered to me, "Be brave." I sat at our table wondering what would happen to give me an opportunity to demonstrate my courage. I did not have long to wait. As we passed the English-style teakettle around and added cream and sugar, and put jam or butter on our biscuits, he began to speak, and we all dispensed with our busyness and gave him our full attention.

"Now, Martin and Eleanor," Jal said. "Your marriage took place back in the States, and it was the marriage of Illusion. Now that you have come here to India and *jumped* out of the Well of Illusion, it's time for you to dissolve that marriage and instead be Best Friends. And when you return to America, continue to be just that—Best Friends!"

In a second, my heart sank through its floorboards. What about all that had happened? What about the key being turned? Anything else I could handle, but Jal's suggestion undermined all that had materialized to indicate to me that I was on the right path in life. My beautiful wife—the very fact that we were together legitimized my life in my own eyes!

Everyone was looking at me, and I needed to respond. All I could do was lift my big cup of tea and mimic Jal's words in a very loud voice: *"Best Friends!"* I began clinking cups with everyone, turning the gathering into a mad hatter's tea party. The others seemed happy to clink and laugh with me. Inside, though, I knew this clowning was merely a form of denial. I had used it to opt out of really feeling the sobering truth, as I was completely unable to let it into my heart.

7.

Two days later we said our goodbyes to Jal and to the Johnsons, who were staying on in India. We took the train, the Deccan Queen, back to Mumbai. Eleanor agreed to keep trying in our marriage—to see if we could be "best friends" who were also husband and wife.

I remember literally nothing from our flight back to America, nor from our drive back to Miami Beach. However, I recall a brief vignette that occurred when we got back to Eleanor's car in the outdoor area of long-term parking at Kennedy airport. Before getting in, we both turned around to look one last time at the sweep of sky just turning to dusk, and at the terminals and runways. We found ourselves facing the main hangar of the airline that had just deposited us back in America. The Japan Airlines building was topped by an enormous, red-lettered neon sign that seemed to be winking at us. It said JAL.

8.

In Miami Beach, we resumed our lives—or rather, Eleanor did. I didn't have a routine to resume, having only arrived there a couple of weeks before our departure for India. While Eleanor worked during the days at the Ocean Sun, I tried to live the life of a writer. I felt raw inside, like a newborn infant, due to the transformative experiences of the past couple of months. I didn't see how I could survive in any kind of workplace.

Sometimes our companionship with one another was relaxed and easy. Other times it was intense, but in what seemed a beautiful way. One day on a lunch visit to chic Collins Avenue, the sidewalks were so crowded that the two of us got separated. This, of course, was long before cell phones existed. I felt my separateness from and union with my beloved like separateness from and union with God. When we were back together in love, it seemed as if God was whole! His proximity felt so immanent that it seemed as though we were having a "higher-plane" experience.

But under the surface, things were not that simple. I had told Eleanor once, in our early days, *"I need all your love."* This had seemed innocent and true at the time, and she had assented, although that was before time and events revealed to us what such a promise really entailed. Though I'd felt justified in making the demand, I've since come to realize how infantile it was.

I became extremely jealous of Ricardo, a handsome Cuban who worked at the Ocean Sun. Through Eleanor, he'd become interested in Baba. The two of them had been good friends before I'd arrived. I have no reason to believe their relationship was anything but platonic, but I was simply helpless to assuage my feelings of jealousy.

Naturally, my wife was not pleased by this. The real breaking point between the two of us, though, arrived one Sunday afternoon when we were at the beach. Two little children started playing with Eleanor. I could not help feeling jealous of them, too! Still believing myself entitled to "all her love," I asked my wife to stop playing with them. Inside I felt like a dark, smoldering mass. My pathetic attempt to control my wife's behavior with the children was the last straw. A few days later, she informed me that I had to leave.

9.

Eleanor was kind enough to let me stay on the living room sofa until I actually left town. I had decided to go to Key West. She and I both believed that although I had "walked 10,000 miles in my moccasins," as she'd put it, since we'd been together, I still wasn't really comfortable with life and people, and needed more "seasoning." For several years, Eleanor herself had lived out a lot of her wild oats in a resort town in the Southwest, before she had come to the point where she could say to me—before the key had been turned, of course—"God is my only lover for the rest of my life."

Out of the blue one day, while I was still camped out on her sofa, she and I were talking and I mentioned San Francisco, in connection with a year I'd spent there in the early '70s. The two words instantaneously "took me there." I didn't *see* San Francisco, but I heard and felt what I knew was the mighty energy of that city, all hundreds or thousands or millions of mega-whatevers, as if I had been *swallowed* by the vast dynamo of its subtle and mental spheres.

10.

I changed my plans and soon departed on the three-day bus journey the west coast, along the southern route. I did not consciously feel devastated about leaving Eleanor. By this time, I had accepted what I could not change.

I half-watched out the window as green Florida went by, looking less and less tropical as we travelled north. The changing terrain accompanied a slide show in my mind: the "mystical" process of our coming together, the cataclysmic emotional work we'd done, our pilgrimage to India. We'd been through *so* much, in just a few months. It had been kind of a whirlwind.

And yet, now it appeared that Meher Baba, whom I *had* to believe was guiding things, wanted me somewhere else. "Someone" had even given me an internal experience to tell me where that was.

Getting out of the bus for a quick dinner in Mobile, Alabama, I *had* to trust that in spite of appearances, my life, with its seeming lack of coherence, was going the way it needed to go. What did "I" as a conscious ego know about when something was over? During his life, Baba had often ended major projects just as his disciples believed they were really getting going. In the spiritual life, something was "over" when the internal work was done. End of story.

I continued to contemplate the trajectory of my life, alternating this with reading, napping, and more gazing, as endless Texas went by. My upbringing had not prepared me for the discontinuities of my recent situation, so I had to stake everything on Baba. The "mystical experiences" I'd been given were no doubt vouchsafed to instill a depth of conviction within me that would endure through times like this.

I did not know if I was capable of obeying Baba as his closest disciples did. I might even have taken a wrong turn somewhere, or many wrong turns, without knowing it. Whatever the case, I knew no other way forward than to "take Baba's name," as He suggested, and keep plowing ahead.

At my first fateful "meeting" with the Master in early 1971, everything in the room and beyond had "filled with Baba" and I had experienced that in reality God alone exists. Since then, not even my own existence as Martin had seemed so incontrovertible.

We turned north after crossing the California desert. In a few hours, a new chapter of my life would begin. I had nothing but a duffel bag, a guitar, and my awareness. I would step off the bus with faith, still fresh from having laid my head upon the tomb of the current Avatar, which Baba had called "the powerhouse of the universe," and having spent two weeks with that Avatar's younger brother, who'd assured me time and again that the world is just a dream.

We would see what kind of dream awaited next.

Falling Off The Map

Part One: Kessler

1.

Something whizzes by my head and on beyond, as I sit on the floor holding the pale green bars of the cell. I twist my neck and see that a flaming wooden match has landed behind me, just in front of the aluminum toilet.

I glance across the small cell block, which the others proudly say once housed a famous group called the San Quentin Six. Kessler is facing me but kneeling on one knee, head down, concentrating on something he's doing. I stand up in order to see. As it all comes into view, I feel a chill. Kessler, his tall, wiry body poised adroitly in his orange prison jumpsuit, is using some kind of charcoal—more matchheads, for all I know—to draw a large, circumscribed *pentangle* on the floor in the center of his cell.

"Kessler, did you throw that match?" I ask.

He tilts his head up until his eyes, looking straight ahead, meet mine. Dark shadows seem to emanate from deep inside them. I feel another chill at this echo of ancient Teutonic magic being practiced across the aisle, seemingly directed against me.

"I'm going to break you!" Kessler announces in a cold voice redolent of an emotion I reluctantly recognize as hatred.

2.

(Font change indicates flashback.)

It started so innocently. I was living an enchanted life here in San Francisco, shortly after my first pilgrimage to Meher Baba's tomb in India. In my mind I would hear Baba's brother Jal's words, repeated over and over to me as he'd done in Pune: *"Everything is false Illusion! Only Baba is real!"*

A month after our return, Eleanor kicked me out in Miami Beach. I planned to go to Key West. We stayed friends, and she let me sleep on her sofa until it was time to leave. A week before my departure, I happened to mention the year I spent in San Francisco at the beginning of the decade. As soon as the name escaped my lips, I started hearing and feeling the mighty vortex of that city's energy. It was as if I was *there,* without being able to see it. I seemed to be having some kind of "subtle experience."

I took this occurrence as a sign and changed my plans. I bought a Greyhound bus ticket and for three days rode west along the southern route, then north to the Bay Area. I spent the whole first day in the city walking around, first from the bus terminal up to Market Street, where I fancied I could still feel distant echoes of the Gold Rush; and later through Golden Gate Park, Haight-Ashbury, and North Beach.

At the edge of Chinatown around 7 pm, I noticed that the sun was starting to sink. I still had no place to stay. I made a quick "Zen" decision. I'd check in to the first affordable place my eyes lit upon.

On the block across Kearny Street from where I stood, across an alley from the 20-storey Holiday Inn, was an old brick building divided into storefronts. Sandwiched between pairs of these storefronts were green doors, apparently leading to residential units on the second floor. Over one of them, an awning bore the words, "Amparo's Hotel."

Idyllic months followed in a foreign land inside the USA, cocooned within its matrix of indecipherable singsong voices. The hotel was more of a rooming-house, really, but it was adequate. Each morning I'd breakfast in one of the little Chinese bakeries, enjoying the exotic delicacies, coffee, and a newspaper. Afterwards, I'd sit there sipping more coffee while reading or writing in a notebook. Later on most mornings, I'd take a walk to a museum, park, waterfront, library, or gallery. Sometimes I'd sit on a bench and feed the pigeons in postage-stamp Portsmouth Park, where the men gathered to do Tai Chi and play checkers. A little after noon, I'd walk back to my room for a nap and a painting session. I scarcely spoke to a soul. It felt as if I was living in Baba's Silence.

After several months, a letter came from a friend in St. Louis, my hometown, bringing news, or at least a rumor, that Reverend Clara was being transferred out here, to San Francisco, to work at some kind of shelter. I smiled as I read this. Reverend C was one of my closest friends from the Holy Order of MANS, the little mystical Christian group I'd discovered in St. Louis, which had been my "surrogate Baba group" before actual Baba meetings had started there.

3.

Weeks later, I walk across town to see if the rumor is true. I'm wearing a brown, moth-eaten sweater that I got at Goodwill. My face is bearded after months of urban hermitage. I approach the front desk at Trinity House, where the letter said she'd be working with battered women and their children. There's an adjoining café called Monk's Bread, where I'd stopped for coffee once, a couple months back.

Reverend C comes walking down the corridor in her sky-blue tunic. Even before I'd known who the sisters of the Order were, I'd always felt inspired to see them walking in pairs, dressed in those tunics, making their way through even the toughest parts of St. Louis as living witnesses to God's beauty and peace.

Reverend C has a huge smile on her face, I notice. Same as mine, no doubt. We slide into one another's arms. After it ends, I wonder, can our embrace really have lasted five minutes? I can feel envy coming from one brother standing nearby, but who can blame him?

4.

I'm afraid, but also curious. Can Kessler really do it? Is there anything *to* this pentangle magic? I've heard of such things since the '60s, but have never seen it practiced. Part of me—a large part—*wants* to be "broken." I mean, isn't that what life is doing to me anyway, especially throughout these last weeks in City Prison, after I kicked the cop?

Being broken: Isn't that what I signed up for, these last eight years since I first felt Meher Baba's Love emanating from His picture and realized that all are one? Various names are used: discipleship, "elimination of the ego." But doesn't it all amount to being broken?

Since my rash kick to the cop's knee, I've felt *someone* has been breaking me. *Killing* me, with a rusty knife, and has left the knife in! I'm an open wound longing for the job to be finished! It might as well be Kessler doing it.

5.

Reverend Clara and I go out to a Russian deli a few blocks away and talk for two hours, sharing memories of the spiritual community I'd felt mystically drawn to in St. Louis. No Baba group existed there when I'd returned in later '75, and I'd longed for some spiritual companions. Walking one day in midtown, I'd come upon a new health food store. The vibes in the place felt exceptional, in fact so good that the word *pure* came to my mind.

As I browsed, the proprietor appeared from the back. I was surprised to find he was an acquaintance from high school! He'd been something of a troubled person back then, and in fact the last time I'd seen him, he had come into a restaurant where I briefly ran a juice bar and asked me to juice two pounds of organic cherries, saying "Maybe this will help me get rid of my bad karma." Now, four or so years later, he seemed solid and shining, like his store.

"Do you belong to a spiritual group?" I spontaneously asked him. He smiled and beckoned for me to come behind the counter. There, he pointed to a sepia picture of Jesus that looked almost like a photograph, taped to the cash register. As I looked, the picture started *glowing* rather intensely. And that was how I found the "surrogate Baba group" that I frequently hung out with for the next beautiful year and a half.

Many of the Order's members were former hippies, like a lot of the "Baba-Lovers" I knew. I even "saw Baba" at one of the group's meetings! Prior to Reverend C's coming, the community was led by four sisters who lived in a little ranch house on the southeast side of the city. Services were held there on Sunday mornings. One day Sister Rose, a dark-haired, attractive woman who smoked a large wooden pipe as she gave her sermons, read us the New Testament passage for the week, the well-known one in which Jesus says, "Tear down this Temple and I will build it up again in three days."

Sister Rose pointed to her body and said, "*This* is your temple."

As I watched, I suddenly saw Meher Baba's head and face, instead of hers, atop her shoulders! It happened instantaneously. Baba was around 35 years old, the age when his physical appearance was the most striking. The vision remained totally clear for around 10 seconds, and then Sister Rose's features reappeared.

Recovering my composure after the shock, all I could think was: those words must be deeply true. They must be so important for me, personally, to remember, that Baba actually *appeared,* to lend emphasis.

Halfway through that year and a half, the community reorganized and Reverend C came to lead it. I had a few counseling sessions with her during this time. At one of them—to defeat the tendency for counseling sessions to be somber and staid—I sat on her lap as we talked! There was no standing on ceremony with these folks. They embodied the humor and lightness of the Living God!

6.

After Reverend C and I part on the day of our reunion, I go back to my hermit life. I bury the thought of her when it comes up. We're platonic friends, I say to myself. I'll see her again "sometime." Pretending to a detachment I don't have, I try to deny that my feelings are intensifying even without conscious sanction.

Occasionally in life, when powerfully attracted to a woman, I've become emotionally paralyzed, unable to either approach or let go. Deep inside, I seem to feel the risk of rejection is too great to chance facing it, even though my denial makes things worse.

This now begins to happen with Reverend Clara. I finally feel compelled to go to the phone on the wall in the rooming house hallway. Dialing, however, I feel a stab of terror, and "someone" inside me stronger than my conscious will won't let me finish.

This battle rages several times over the next month. Never able to complete the call, I go on with my daily routine, but no longer with such a carefree heart. Sometimes, now I feel lost. I believe God is with me, and often continue to feel His presence. But often now, too, what Jal had called "the Illusion"—in this case, of loneliness and need—begins to overwhelm me. I try hard to stay creatively busy, but sometimes am unsuccessful.

One night, I do my best to be creative with the isolation itself. I personify the needy part of me as if "it" is one of the suffering lepers or *masts* (God-mad souls) whom Meher Baba cared for during his ministry. The remaining parts of me—head, arms, and upper body—I decide, will be "Baba." The "Baba" in me literally *bathes* the sufferer in me.

Such unconventional acts, in the face of growing emotional isolation and helplessness, are sometimes the best my wits and intuition can come up with. I'm not really sure whether they help or not.

7.

"Vermin like you don't deserve to live!" Kessler's angry words abruptly rouse me from my latest reverie. "Starting at noon tomorrow, when you least expect it, there will be more matches whizzing by your head! Landing in your clothes! I'll scream at you so you can't sleep, harass you until you beg for mercy! I won't leave you alone!"

"Have you ever 'broken' anyone before?" I ask, a bit frightened now.

"In Vietnam," he says. *"Gooks."* His tone of voice carries an implication that "gooks" are not people. I'm not sure he believes I'm a person, either.

8.

Earlier on that fateful evening of "the kick," I'm sitting on a curb out on Grant Avenue amid the hubbub of strolling tourists, traffic, and Chinese-language hawkers. I'm already a bit degenerate, having just pulled a Styrofoam container out of the trash. Living a solitary life around here, it's easy to get into such a habit.

Opening the container, I see two nearly pristine Egg Foo Yung patties. One of them has a tiny bite taken out of it. The other is like new. Why are people so wasteful? I pick the first one up and bring it to my mouth to taste, then wolf both down in a few bites.

Loud trumpet tones blare from somewhere nearby. I turn my head and see a thin African-American man in a suit, blowing jazz, his trumpet case open in front of him with a few bills and some coins lying on its plush purple. Just one more sound in the cacophony here. But suddenly—and who knows why, at this particular moment—something inside me *snaps*.

I stand up and begin walking, knowing somehow that the life I've been living these past months is over. It's clear I have to walk that half mile to Sutter Street and up its long incline to find her, face her, and tell her how I feel. The feelings have consumed me. I have no choice.

Down the length of Grant, amid laughing couples and paper lanterns, along the congested sidewalk, I stride. Down the steps beside the stone lions at California Street and through the Financial District, then right onto Sutter.

Partway up the hill in the ink-dark night, I realize I need a bathroom. Passing a dirty brown-brick "B" hotel, I walk in the front door and find myself in the small rectangle of the gold-lit lobby. A man behind the counter is talking to a customer. I look around, but fail to spot a "Restroom" sign.

"Where's the *shithouse*?" I demand, walking up beside the tourist.

"This is no way to talk!" shouts the clerk in a European-inflected voice, as he makes a very sour face.

"I need the shithouse!" I demand again, far past all moorings now, refusing to honor the lies that comprise polite euphemistic language. The man shakes his head disgustedly, apologizes to his customer, and points towards a winding, tiled stairway at the end of the lobby. I walk towards it, descend, and relieve myself. Returning, I pad back through the lobby and out again into the shadows, without a word.

It's several more blocks up the long hill and then down a bit, to Trinity House. Approaching the lighted building, I pull open the door and enter without hesitation.

"I need to see Reverend Clara! I need to see her," I tell the young man at the desk. "My name is Martin."

9.

I think back to my first days in the cell block after recovering, somewhat, from the initial shock of incarceration. Being here is one of those things I believed could not happen to me. Settling into this life after the first few days, though, I began to think that maybe I *can* "bring Meher Baba with me," as he said to do wherever we go. Bring him even here—more than simply repeating his name internally, which I've continued to do. Life goes on, on the far side of *whatever* once seemed unimaginable, including, no doubt, even death—until you finally, in some lifetime, *become* the Life Eternal that is all that truly exists.

I'd tried to tell the guys on this cell block about Baba: Kessler, lethargic Davey with his "white Afro" in the cell next to him, and massive, muscle-laden Ray in *his* orange jumpsuit, a professional football player of some kind, in the cell down by the block's entrance.

I don't remember how the moment came when I was able to bring up Baba naturally. Maybe it was Bill's complaining once more that there are no TVs in the cells here, and no cheese puffs and chips, all of which he apparently had free access to during a previous incarceration somewhere.

I'd seized the opportunity to try to inspire my fellow inmates. I'd read once about a soldier in the Indian army during India's war with China in 1962. Deep in enemy territory, he had inspired his comrades to great bravery by telling them about Meher Baba, the God-Man. Afterward, his whole platoon had been motivated to call on Baba with all their hearts, and they'd safely made their way through enemy territory and back to India against enormous odds.

I'd spoken up in what may have seemed a *non sequitur* to the others, hoping the force of my words could make it fit into the group conversation. "There was a man named Meher Baba, who lived a life like Buddha or Christ in India recently, and did spiritual work that will change everything on Earth! He said his work will raise human consciousness from Reason to Intuition. His life was absolutely selfless. He worked with the poor, the mentally ill ... and once, while visiting America, he had himself driven to the gates of Sing Sing prison, to make inner contact with an inmate."

Bill and Ray had tried to shout me down, but Kessler, the natural leader of the group, had shushed them. "Listen to him!" Kessler had admonished. "He's saying something important!"

How had things degenerated? In the end, I hadn't been able to stay bravely in my heart like the Indian soldier. The noise of the whole prison, which could be heard in our block; the 24-hour lights; the endless chatter of the guys near me, who were like boys who'd never outgrown their games of cops and robbers—all of it had been too much. I'd remained a middle-class, Jewish suburban mama's boy. By now, no doubt, I was clinically depressed. I longed for Kessler to carry out his plan. Anything that would deliver me from the chaos that reigned in my mind.

10.

Coming down the corridor on my second visit, Reverend Clara isn't smiling.

"*I want to make love to you!*" I say, somewhat relieved to declare myself, even as I remain unable to wrap myself back up in appropriate language.

She responds with three words: "I'm getting married."

Her mention of marriage immediately fills me with guilt at what I've already said. It's too late to take that back, but my raw need and desire quickly slide underground. I realize she hasn't been idle during the weeks I've spent wrestling with the telephone. I've known that the sisters and brothers of the Order observe a year of celibacy, after which they're free to marry. Was she already engaged at the time of our first reunion? I sense the answer is no, but that's water under the bridge. All I can do now, if I care at all about her, is express my support.

"That's wonderful!" I say, a happy well-wisher now. "Well, will you come to our deli haunt and let me get you a sandwich to celebrate?"

"OK," she says in what seems a friendly tone. "Go on over. I'll be along in a little while."

Back out in the night, I wonder at this turn of events. Will I be able to cope? Two or three minutes later I push open the door of the deli and sit down at a table. No other customers in the place. I pick up a San Francisco Chronicle that's been left on another table, and glance at the front page: *January 31, 1979*, it says under the thick black headline that reads **Khomenei Returning to Iran.**

Today is Amartithi! It's the 10th anniversary of the day Meher Baba died—dropped his body, as close disciples say. What a strange coincidence that on this special night I feel myself breaking inside, watching all my bridges collapse.

After 15 minutes, it begins to sink in that she isn't coming. She's afraid. Why didn't she just say so? Maybe she intended to come, but then a supervisor ordered her not to. I pick myself up and walk out yet again, the bells on the deli door jingling behind me.

Back in the lobby alcove at Trinity House, the desk man is quite stern. I stand there, not knowing what to do. A tall, kind-looking brother in the brown tunic that the men wear comes and stands, facing me, in front of the security table. "You really need to leave now," he says. "If you don't, I'll be forced to call the police and have them arrest you for trespassing."

This isn't at all what I had in mind. I really did just want to get her a congratulatory meal and to part as friends.

I walk away from the brother, into a large, dimly-lit room to the side of the alcove. Looking up, I see a dome with beautiful stained glass and a circle of gilded, painted angels up near the top. Back at the security table, I can hear someone dialing a telephone and then speaking in a low voice.

A few minutes later, the front door opens. Four San Francisco cops in dark blue enter the room and stand near me. Two have mustaches. They look like giants. Guns bulge from the holsters in their belts. The tall young brother comes in and whispers to them. Two other brothers, one with a look of contempt on his face, follow him.

"I'll ask you one more time," says the soft-spoken brother, turning to me. "After that, I'll ask the policemen to escort you out. Please leave right now."

I listen carefully for the voice of Jesus in his voice. The first few words are kind, and I'm ready to go out the door like a lamb, but as I prepare to comply, his voice pulls back. I hear a trace of enmity. He's *not* detached. He doesn't understand, and he can't completely disguise it. We stand there, a tableau under the timeless angels high above. I wait for a moment, to see once more if someone will ask me in a spirit of genuine brotherhood, but no one says another word.

I give the tall young brother a push—not hard, it's only symbolic, but so that he feels it. Two cops move forward to grab me. As they do so, I kick one of them in the shin.

Suddenly, the policemen are lightning in the form of bodies, springing toward me, all four of them, 25 feet of height and probably 900 pounds! They grab my arms, legs, back, and stomach, and pull me out onto the dark and noisy street. They slam me onto the sidewalk and rapidly cuff my hands behind my back. It's all over, almost before it began. I lie there hog-tied, in the ruins of my life.

11.

I continue to wait for Kessler to put his plans into action. When noon, or approximately noon, comes the next day, my expectancy rises. But nothing happens. Nothing happens that night, either, or the next day. The day after that, I get up my nerve and address Kessler.

"*What happened?*" I demand. It's obvious that he isn't carrying out his avowed program.

"I decided you weren't worth it," he says curtly. It's the ultimate snub. I'm not even worth breaking.

Things begin to happen very quickly a couple of days after Kessler's dropping of his plan. At around 10 in the morning, the guards come to take him away. He's been using a set of law books that he's had on a shelf up on his wall, pursuing some kind of appeal. Today the verdict came in. He lost.

"Pack your things and be ready in half an hour," the guard warns. Right on schedule, they're back.

"You can't do this!" Kessler shouts. But they can, and they do. They carry him out, and in another minute he's gone, as if he'd never been there.

The day after that, word comes that I, too, am leaving. Lindstrom, the big-bodied, green-uniformed guard who seems to detest me more than he detests the bank robbers and murderers, comes to tell me I need to be ready in 30 minutes. I'm being sent to Napa State Hospital for observation.

Bill and Ray don't even say goodbye. Tom, a shy, bearded fellow who joined us recently, rumored to be charged with arson after a fire in his rooming house, and whom I'd tried to stand up for when the others had taunted him about being gay, looks my way and nods.

I'm still not "broken." "Baba," I say inwardly to the One I continue to try, at least, to make my constant companion. *"When will it all end?"*

As usual, these days, I hear no reply.

Part Two: Limbo

1.

Napa State Hospital
After the van dropped me off here and I went through intake, I was allowed to phone my parents to tell them my new location. "Hey, that's wine country!" Dad said in an attempt at humor. The view from the picture window in the day room does happen to be spectacular. It looks out on fields and vineyards, and behind them layer upon layer of hills, all in more shades of green than I've ever imagined. But the hospital is not a tourist resort. It's more like a mansion of neglect. The cavernous gymnasium has been transformed into a huge dorm filled with green cots. I guess this is the only way they can accommodate everyone.

Though I'm supposedly here for observation, I haven't yet noticed anyone observing me. There's little supervision of any sort. It's been a week since I arrived, and I haven't had a single interaction with medical or psychiatric personnel. There aren't even many orderlies.

A skinny, long-haired inmate who resembles Tiny Tim walks around every morning with a beat-up guitar, playing and singing the rock song "Gloria" to wake everyone up. A ragtag entourage follows him, and their shouts of "G-L-O-R-I-A!" get almost all the late-risers off their cots. It's rather charming.

In the day room, against Nature's gorgeous backdrop, an inmate named Rocky monopolizes everyone's attention with a never-ending narrative of his past exploits. A Seventh-day Adventist, he relates everything he says to "Jehovah God."

One day Rocky's not there. The scuttle is that he's escaped. The next day he's back, holding forth once more. His latest adventure and new notoriety don't improve his storytelling skills, and I decide to avoid the day room. With only a little exploration, I discover there are small rooms, with their brick walls painted in institutional light green, that no one ever goes in. It's possible to actually get some privacy!

I lie on a beanbag pillow that's in one of these rooms, looking at a painting on the wall, of a man fishing in a lake. After a while, the rod starts to bend. It appears the man's hooked a fish! What's going on?

Things begin appearing on the walls, too. Are these hallucinations? There isn't anything scary about them. The wall images a bit sad, though. The pattern of brick and mortar morphs somehow into a kind of animated cartoon. I see a swamp, a great sad swamp with big cypress trees, their lower trunks sunk in the water. A figure in a little rowboat is plying the waters, propelling the boat with an oar or a pole. The figure looks something like Winnie-the-Pooh. He's extremely forlorn—just so *lonely*—as he continues to pole through the monotonous swamp. Wherever he goes looks just like where he's been. It seems there's no end to this, and no one anywhere to help, or even to meet or see.

It doesn't require higher math to solve the equation of whom this forlorn figure might represent. Will I ever get out of this limbo? Since that night in the city, I've felt as if I've slipped underground into some kind of parallel world. This began as soon as the police tackled me. I don't know how to assimilate it all. Memories come at night, as I'm lying on my cot in the silent gymnasium, trying to fall asleep.

2.

I'm taken in a van to the Hall of Justice on Brannon Street south of Market, fingerprinted and photographed, and then led to a large holding cell that's part of San Francisco City Prison, located in the building's basement.

This cell holds at least 25 men, maybe as many as 50—all kinds of men, but many are "biker types," big, bearded, and motorcycle-jacketed. A lot of them are sitting around a great oaken table in the center of the cell. They're making a tremendous din! It all seems more like a celebration than a sober response to having been arrested. The whole scene feels like something out of ancient times, like the publicans in the days of Christ.

I have no idea how to behave in this milieu. There's a paperback novel in my jacket pocket, one I began a few days ago. I find a little space on the bench that hugs the bars all the way around the cell, and sit down to read. The noise, though, makes sustained concentration impossible.

Sitting there, I realize a few things. My kick and subsequent arrest were certainly a catastrophe, but however calamitous they may have been, I've now recovered a sense of Meher Baba's presence. I also know I'll lose that in this chaos if I'm here long. It will drive me mad. There seems to be no way to think, meditate, or calm the mind.

Internally, I ask Baba what to do. The seeming answer comes from the pages of my novel, The Lost Weekend, which is about a man's recovery from chronic alcoholism. In the section I've just finished, the protagonist has been on a binge. Sober again and contemplating the ruins of his life, he, too, has had a realization: "No one is going to do it for me. The only one who can do anything about my situation is me."

But what can I do in my situation? I know I have a legal right to a phone call, and so far I haven't been offered one. If I call my parents in Missouri, they'll surely bail me out. But I'm just not ready to tell them what's happened. The evening has left me too shaken up and ashamed.

There's only one way I can think of to get out of this cell. It seems absurd, but no matter how many times I go over things in my mind, nothing else comes. The idea is this: If I wade into the crowd with my fists flying, someone will probably call the guards and they'll put me in solitary.

I've never been one to fight, even in childhood, but the courage to at least mock-fight is what I believe the situation demands. I may not have been brave enough to risk possible rejection and phone Reverend Clara, but the consequences of that have already occurred. "Now" goes on. In this "Now," a terrible new challenge seems to loom.

I stop thinking. The time has come for action. I say Baba's Name to myself, stash my book in a pocket, and walk forward toward the center of the cell, fists flailing indiscriminately at the bodies I pass. I make sure not to look at faces, only try to land the punches.

After a little while I hear someone shout, "Guard, guard!" I keep on slugging, but before long, two burly guards noisily open and enter the cell. They grab me and pin my arms behind my back. A young man with a wounded expression comes up in front of me and shouts to the guards, "He just walked by me and hit me! I didn't do *anything*!"

The guards push me forward, out of the cell. One of them leads me to an elevator, to another floor, and then down a corridor. He opens up a door and says, "Chill out here awhile." I enter, and he closes and locks the cell door. My plan has worked.

I have no sense of the sequence of time after that. The solitary cell feels like a precious blessing. I can think! Three times a day, meals are delivered by a prison "trustee." One of them looks at me in a tender way as he brings my tray of eggs, toast and coffee the next morning, and exclaims, "Soon we'll be in paradise!" before exiting and locking the door. Was he some kind of angel?

Sometimes it's impossible to tell whether it's day or night. At a certain point, though, they do turn most of the lights off, so that it's possible to sleep.

My second night in solitary, one of the strangest experiences in my life takes place. I'm sitting there thinking, meditating, and "talking to Baba," when suddenly, a beam of light begins to project from each of my eyes, as from a movie projector. An image takes form on the wall a couple of feet in front of me. On this "screen," I watch a scene unfold.

A couple is walking through the desert, to the village well. They appear to be betrothed. They are dressed in apparel that seems to indicate they live in the Middle East. The woman is balancing a large water pot on her head.

As they reach the well, another figure appears, coming up over a large sand dune. His bearded face appears first, then the rest of him. He is wearing a white robe trimmed with red. He beckons to the young betrothed couple. The young woman runs to him immediately.

The young man, on the other hand, takes a step toward him, then hesitates. He retakes the same step and then hesitates again. He continues to do this, repeating the action several times, yet getting no further. Then the scene begins to dissolve. The "beams" from my eyes quickly disappear, and the room is back to normal.

What did I just see? Clearly, the man coming over the hill was Jesus. Was the younger man "me" in a past life? I flash on someone who, I get a hunch, might have been the young woman. I intuit that the young man is just too attached to his life, possibly involved in his father's business.

How can something like this happen? Where am I in the great stream of life, and where can I go from here? How can I get out of here? I call out to Meher Baba from the deepest reaches of my heart, as I've regularly done ever since my first experience of Him eight years ago.

Of course, no one comes to deliver me, and the next day the guard who brought me to solitary returns and walks me to the cell block that will be my home for the next month or so.

3.

After another week at Napa, I'm told to report to the loading area again. It's late in the day. This time, I'm the only passenger in the van. Night has fallen by the time we arrive back in downtown San Francisco. We're not near the Hall of Justice, but on the other side of Market. I hear sirens nearby, as you so often do at night in the city. We're pulling alongside a large building that looks like Saint Francis Hospital, and in a moment I see a sign confirming that it is.

The van drives into the garage and parks. I'm led into the building, to a tiny room with a bed, where I lie for several hours, totally disoriented, with no clue as to what's going on. Finally, someone comes and says, "It's time to go." We walk back to the van and it drives through the city some more. Half an hour later, it pulls into yet another hospital garage.

"Where are we?" I ask the uniformed man leading me inside.

"St. Mary's." He takes me to another room with a bed. This one is a little bigger. By now it's late at night, and I climb into the bed and go to sleep.

St. Mary's, it turns out, is adjacent to the Haight-Ashbury district and close to Golden Gate Park, at the other end of the city from downtown. As with all such institutions, it embodies its own variations on the general theme. The floor which constitutes the psych ward is a study in modernity, the opposite of Napa. The day room here, the environment in which patients are expected to spend much of their waking time, is an enormous, impersonal, and windowless cavern in the center of the ward. Entering the vast room the day after my arrival, I feel I've been swallowed up like a speck. I have an impulse to go and look for myself. Furthermore, once in here, there isn't much to do. I no longer have a good book, and may not even have enough concentration left to read. I don't care for cards, puzzles or daytime TV.

I'm sitting alone at a table wondering how to pass the time, when two people around my age approach me. "Hi, I'm Ruth!" says one of them. I look up and see a tall woman with black hair and bright red lipstick.

"I'm Chris!" says a curly-haired man in a maroon sweater. Chris has a rather severe rash on his face, and he's smiling—big! Ruth smiled, too, during her greeting, but Chris just keeps his toothy smile, as if it's frozen on his face.

From then on, the three of us become companions, almost as if we're on a ball-and-chain gang, by virtue of the fact that there's no one else remotely near our age and capable of interacting.

"I work for the *Chronicle,*" Ruth says. She sounds as if she may be telling the truth. She's intelligent, well-dressed, and has the "grown-up" appearance a Chronicle reporter might. She has one trait, though, which unnerves me and makes me unable to imagine anyone wanting to be around her much. To almost anything you say to her, she replies with, "No, actually..." and then goes on to set you straight about how things *really* are.

Chris says he's a street performer. He does a card trick for us. Then he begins sliding cards around in a Three-Card Monte manner. I don't know what he did that got him into this place, but I get the feeling he's been on the street a lot, maybe living there.

After a couple of days Ed, the bearded orderly who tries very hard not to disturb anyone as he pads from place to place, brings a new patient into the day room, an Asian boy who is probably 12 or 13 years old. He's dressed in jeans and a dark button-up shirt. Ed introduces him as Pak.

Pak speaks no English at all. He works on a puzzle Ed has given him, alone at a small table. But after awhile, he abruptly stands up, walks a little way forward, and looks like he's about to enter some kind of a runway. You can feel there's a whole world of invisible objects and people he's bringing here from memory. He stands before some sort of imagined audience, raises a fist in the air, and shouts, *"Pak wing chow!"* After a little while, he walks down the imagined runway. Then the scenario dissipates, and he goes and sits down again and resumes working on his puzzle. He repeats this ritual every hour or so.

I have the impression that Pak's behavior is more of a cultural than a psychiatric phenomenon, and that there's just no other place for them to put him. As he speaks no English, I'm not able to find out anything definite. I could ask Ed for more information, but I'm not exactly on top of the world, myself, and it would take more energy than I have.

Memories from city prison keep coming back, at night, when I'm alone in my room.

4.

A wispy, bearded fellow named Tom has joined us in our cell block. He's gay, or at least the other inmates say he is, and taunt him about it at night. They also say he burned down his rooming house, and they make noises like the ghost of the person they say died in the fire. I don't really know if *any* of their patter is true, but one day during the half hour we get for exercise, I'm down at the far end beside the cell of Ray, the tall, muscular guy who is, or was, a pro football player. He shouts, "Fairy!" as Tom passes by. I walk into Ray's cell and say, "Why don't you leave Tom alone? You know, we all have a female side; we all have a gay person inside us!"

I'm kind of proud that I've spoken up, but before I know it, Ray, without saying a word, shoves his huge fist like lightning into the side of my face! I fall down, almost into his cell's toilet. But the funny thing is, I'm *laughing*! I'm laughing because—because it doesn't hurt! I've almost never been hit in the face, in my life. Whatever fear I might have had of it, I realize, was ridiculous! It happened so fast! The sensation was so clean, somehow, that it was practically fun!

Nevertheless, from now on, I'll think twice about even talking to Ray.

Another day, at exercise time, I'm allowed to walk in the area beyond our cell block. A husky, mustached fellow in a red prison jumpsuit joins me as I pace. He starts talking to me, putting an arm around me as if he's my older brother. He says, "They got nothin' on me! They say I killed this guy and buried him in the landfill. I been here six months. I got my lawyers on it. You stick with me, I'll take care of you."

Exercise period ends after he's gone on for about 15 minutes. I've held back the one question I wanted to ask: "Well, *did* you kill him?" But who's going to ask a possible murderer a question like that? That's the way it is in here. The threat of violence lies behind just about every relationship. It's yet another force working to shut a person down.

Another memory, from the "enchanted" period before "the kick," is almost unbelievable now. Yet it's just how it was!

One night, near the end of that life, I'm jogging through the city and go into an open Texaco station to ask the night attendant if I might use the bathroom. He's a nice-looking English fellow about my age. His name is Eden Hutton. We strike up a conversation, and I mention Baba to him. Eden is clearly a seeker of Truth. I was able to sense it after just a little while. I invite him to visit me at my rooming house sometime, and a few evenings later, he comes.

There's a particular reason I want him to come. He's a nice fellow, in fact just about the only real friend, or potential friend, I feel I've made during my six months in the city. I want him to feel what I feel in my room: the wall!

I have one entire wall covered with posters of Meher Baba and glorious nature photos that also feature profound Baba quotes, such as, "Love is essentially self-communicative; those who do not have it catch it from those who have it."

The thing is that for several weeks, as I've built this "collection," it's taken on a life of its own. There is Light—there is, in fact, Love—coming off this wall, almost all the time, rising like a great natural force! It bathes me, it feeds me ... and yet, before Eden arrives, no one else has ever been here to see and feel it!

It's like a Wall demarcating the world of form from that further Beyond of God's formless Love! When I lie in bed at night, awash in it, I feel I'm the most fortunate person alive!

Eden comes, and I put on a kettle for tea. While it perks, I take him to the wall. It's not far to go, as the room is small. He stands before it, taking it in. And then I see ... I *see*, with my physical eyes, a *pink cloud* rising up from the wall, or possibly from one of the photos. I watch it hover in the air a bit, *and then go straight down into Eden! Right into the top of his head!*

Exactly *what* did I just witness? Was he aware of it? I refrain from saying anything about what I observed, nor does he mention anything. We have tea and talk a bit, and then he leaves.

Shortly after that comes, well, "the kick." I never see Eden again, and there's a very good chance I never will.

5.

Chris is an unmerciful tease. He's pretty good at his Three-Card Monte, and I'm still near the end of my emotional rope. And that smile of his—grinning like the Cheshire cat, no matter what he's saying or feeling. He makes verbal asides and then just smiles as though someone else has uttered them.

I'm trying to see through his sleight-of-hand one day, as Ruth watches. Suddenly the game seems to turn into some kind of manhood test. I guess wrong a couple more times. He says "Not the brightest light, are we?" I try and miss again, and I begin to feel raw. This time he says, "Afraid to call a girl—at your age! Scaredy-cat! Scaredy-cat!"

I'd confided in him about Reverend Clara, but not in Ruth's presence. Something in me suddenly becomes too much the victim, the bottom dog, for me to bear. I watch my left fist thrust out right into Chris's face.

Emil, the orderly on duty in the day room, immediately calls in an alarm. Three more orderlies came running in. They pin me down—not quite as roughly as the police—but they sit on me so I can't move.

"Sorry," I say recovering a bit. None of these recent behaviors are things I recognize in myself, but how can I explain that?

"You'll be on close watch for 48 hours," Emil says. "Someone will be two feet or less from you at all times."

Tom, my first shadow, is someone I haven't seen much of before. He doesn't brook any nonsense and doesn't seem to have a sense of humor. When his shift ends, Kevin comes on. Kevin is a short Asian fellow who carries a little handbook of Nichiren Buddhism, the sect whose members chant "Nam-Myoho-Renge-Kyo." Kevin is very confident, and espouses a very simple doctrine of Spiritual Reason.

"You just have to keep putting good karmas into life," he says when I ask him about his book. "That will offset all the bad karmas from previous lives." His little discourse leaves me pondering once again how my "bad karmas" got me into this negative cycle, and how to begin again to put in the "good karmas," at which I seem to be failing miserably. Kevin's "reasonable Buddhism" is not really different from what Baba teaches. It sounds so simple and obvious, the way he describes it.

Kevin, though more approachable than Tom, also has to play his strict "shadow" role, and the next two days are among the most unhappily claustrophobic I've ever spent. Having someone I didn't choose in my intimate space gets very old, very fast. I'm allowed to go into the toilet stall itself without my shadow, but he stays right outside. Other than that, he's all but handcuffed to me. He can't enjoy it any more than I do, but he at least gets paid for his effort! Everything they do at St. Mary's seems born of some weird permutations of Reason. However, I will definitely think much more before slugging anyone else, no matter what the provocation.

Finally, 48 hours are up and the shadow is called off. The relief is palpable. Chris and I are back to being friends, as much as you can be friends with someone whose face is confined to one expression. He seems to curb his insults from then on.

Day follows day and week follows week, and the stir-craziness grows.

6.

The stay at St. Mary's lasts much longer than the one at Napa. In fact, there's no clue *how* long I'm going to be there. I'm not sure of my precise legal status or the progress of my case to trial, but it's pretty clear I still have an assault charge pending, and remain a ward of the justice system.

In this venue, I'm at least able to speak regularly with my parents. After I've been here something more than a month, Mother tells me she and Dad have decided she'll fly out and see if there's anything she can do to expedite matters downtown.

She puts up at a smart little hotel on Market Street. For the first couple of days, she shares her suite there with Agnes Baron. Agnes is a longtime disciple of Meher Baba who administers Meher Mount, a property dedicated to Baba that's located outside of Ojai, in southern California. I'd reached out to Agnes by phone from prison once, and in response, she's hitchhiked all the way up to here, at least 300 miles, solely to see me. She comes to the hospital with Mother, and the three of us go out to lunch. I'm not really myself, and haven't been for months, but I'm touched that this busy lady whom I've never met face-to-face before has come such a distance for my benefit.

The next day Agnes has to leave, to get back to her land, but Mom comes to St. Mary's every day. The hospital lets me leave in her company, so long as I'm back by 8 p.m.

I'm still submerged beneath many tons of emotional avalanche, but Mom hasn't come all this way for conversation. She just wants to help, in part because she feels guilty. She believes a lot of my problems in life are due to an abusive atmosphere at her mother's apartment in New York City, where she and Dad lived while she was pregnant with me. Of course, I don't remember being an embryo, and tend to think of my current problems as self-created. Still, I'm glad my parents are actively on my side. You hear all sorts of tales about parents who "wash their hands" of troubled children, and I'm not entirely sure I'd survive that.

At dinner in the Haight, the day after Agnes' departure, Mother says, "The city has a *hold* on you!" She'd been downtown earlier and found that indeed, the justice system has its teeth in me and doesn't want to let go. Either they don't distinguish between "symbolic" kicks to cops and those intended to injure, or else I've become a mere number in a bureaucracy.

After that, when Mom's not with me, she's back down at the Hall of Justice working the case. I've been arraigned on assault charges. There's no guarantee that there's anything at all she can do, beyond taking me to lunch or dinner.

One rainy morning, she and I take a cab and go to visit a couple of psychiatrists who live in the same residential neighborhood. She's trying to salvage my mind as well as get me out of virtual jail. Compared with my mind, though, even the justice system is simple.

We see my assigned St. Mary's doctor at his home. He's an intelligent man who keeps his case notes in a stylishly-worn leather binder and wears patches on the elbows of his sport coats. He also wears a perpetual sneer on his lips that makes me think of Pontius Pilate, and openly scorns anything I say that smacks of spiritual optimism.

Walking the several blocks to the second doctor, I trail behind Mom as if she's a "Show Mother" and I'm her little stage protégé. This second man champions the "orthomolecular" diet that's supposed to re-balance a person with massive doses of Vitamin C. But I'm like a baby chick, just glad to have some warmth from the mother hen.

Another day, I visit her perfect little hotel on Market Street, and we have lunch in an exclusive cafeteria next door. As we're going through the line, I hear the head chef *scream* at a young worker, *"You need more* **red** *in that display!"* It's as if the fellow has committed a capital offense. Yes, that's how it is, I tell myself as we dig into the sumptuous food. Part of me isn't even that anxious to return to such a world.

Mom brings "the good life" with her wherever she goes. It's a comfort, although, unfortunately, a small one.

7.

Finally, the breakthrough in the case arrives, via what seems an unlikely route. My parents haven't been able to make any impression at all on the legal system. No one is interested in taking another look at my case.

As a last resort, Dad phones a man with whom he was close friends way back in his army days, someone who, upon re-entering civilian life, married a San Francisco heiress and became one of the city's best-known philanthropists. Dad hasn't even spoken to him since attending his wedding years before, but decides one day to give him a call and tell him about my predicament. As he continues outlining the bleak situation, he mentions the name of the judge who has been assigned to the case.

"He lives right down the street from me!" is his friend's surprised response. "We're good friends." Soon after, Dad's friend visits his neighbor, the judge, and explains that I've never been in trouble with the police before and that no one was injured by my soft kick.

A few days later, the wheels of the system begin to turn. The charges are dropped. I'm released in the custody of my mother on the condition that I leave the state.

I'm in no condition to object to my release on the grounds that young men from the inner city are not privy to such boons. I accept the unlikely coincidence that has produced this result as divine grace. My release resolves one problem, but I remain deeply depressed by the experiences of the past several months. I don't know whether my sanity, let alone my enthusiasm for life, will ever come back. If I'd remained amid the chaos of either prison or hospital, though, I'm pretty certain there would have been no chance for recovery, at all.

Part Three: Return

1.

Dad picks us up at the airport in St. Louis. I entered the prison system at the end of January, and now it's high summer. After a big embrace with Dad and a stop at a restaurant, we drive the rest of the way to the house where I grew up. Familiarity is a small comfort as I see the maple trees I know so well lining the street, and begin reciting to myself the litany of families' names going up the block.

I enter our large corner house through its heavy oak door. I walk straight up the stairs and get into bed. And basically, I don't get out again for more than a year.

The defeat of the past six months is so profound that I'm totally unable to face the world. Waking each morning as the light enters the room, I close the blinds and lie there with eyes shut. My parents go out to their jobs and come home, and I still haven't moved. I'm always shocked that a whole day has gone by. It always seems like a few hours at most.

Mother and Dad don't interfere, except to stipulate that I visit a psychiatrist weekly. One of them comes home that first day and drives me to the office of an old friend of theirs, a rather aged man whom, I feel, tries to treat me with platitudes. Once I'm back home, I return to bed.

My parents may believe at first, "He'll do this for a week or two and then start living again," but I don't. Continuing my escape through shut-eyed confinement, I daydream or nap-dream, ruminating over the recent past or the distant past, going through various mental scenarios, or indulging in self-deprecating interior monologues—first for those first couple of weeks, then for the rest of the month, and then the month after that and the one after that. My doctor tells me, after a month or so, "You're like a concentration camp survivor who is released, but doesn't get better."

During the evenings, I venture into my parents' bedroom and watch TV with Dad. I detest most of the shows, with their preposterous plots and canned laughter, *Barney Miller* and *Welcome Back, Kotter* being a little better than the rest. I sit on my parents' bed, with Dad nearby in his easy chair. The chaos put out by the TV is nearly as mind-numbing as prison, but I sit here like a little boy because being near Dad in this way is really my only human contact.

On weekend nights, Mother joins us. One Saturday, the film *Midnight Express* comes on after *Saturday Night Live*. It's about a young American incarcerated in a Turkish dungeon. As we watch, I begin to feel myself dissociating from my body. I hadn't known that a film could trigger a psychotic episode, but suddenly I find myself plunged into emotional darkness and panic, psychologically back in city prison! I sit rigidly in front of my parents, until I finally find the words to communicate the nature of my problem. They turn off the TV and put in a call to my doctor. In time, the experience passes.

2.

Around 13 months after my return, some life slowly begins to stir in me. An old friend, who has been phoning occasionally to see if I want to go out for lunch or dinner, calls again. For some reason, this time, I say yes. His gentle companionship is a good re-introduction to the world.

I begin actually getting up in the morning—listening to the Larry King radio show, with its interesting topics and guests. I even phone in once to make a comment. This is a big step beyond lying there with my eyes closed. I begin going for walks and reading books, and attending a weekly discussion group that my friend belongs to.

As recovery progresses, Mother asks me if I want to volunteer at a Montessori-style preschool in an African-American church in the city. A lady she knows from her library job is on the board there, and has mentioned this opportunity. I begin spending a few hours a day at the Ascension Episcopal Church, under the direction of a very wise and kind teacher, Mrs. Alice Esters.

The company of the children is medicine to my spirit. One morning, a few weeks after I've started, as they lay on their cots at Rest Time, a little girl named Tiffany calls out in total innocent trust, "Mr. Martin, I'm *so* glad you're here!"

Her words leave my heart echoing and my eyes wet. I know I've come back from hell.

ALTERNATING CURRENT

Part One

1.

Odds are, reader, you've never had ECT, short for electroconvulsive therapy and colloquially known as shock treatment. If that's so, you may believe it's a form of torture only a step up from lobotomy and maybe a few steps up from the electric chair.

For me, having had a series of treatments, it isn't quite that simple. First of all, for the sake of credibility, my credentials: I'm an upstanding member of my community, married, a teacher and a published author. There were a few years earlier in my life-odyssey, though, during a drawn-out adjustment to adulthood that lasted way into my thirties, when I kept losing the trail. I'd find it for a while and be very tuned in, creative, productive—then it would disappear again, and I'd be off the map, you might say. Getting to know a psychiatric ward, or several of them, is an occupational hazard that comes with being off the map. There simply are no other kinds of refuge in our society for people in certain kinds of distress.

These places aren't so bad, actually, unless they insist on pumping you full of drugs. And back in the early '80s, the period I'm talking about, if you or your parents had "a policy," you could check in to your friendly nearby psych ward for a couple of weeks almost free of charge.

It's surprisingly easy to lose your mental balance, if you're fragile in the first place. We're all like tops spinning with the centrifugal momentum of all our habits, plus the underpinning of our values and everything that's happened before in our lives. How easy it is for a top to be upended!

Here's an example: one time I started to feel overwhelmed by emotional residue from childhood issues that was making its way up from deep inside. These matters had been resolved for the most part, yet remained somewhat raw. There must have been external circumstances throwing me into myself as well, but I don't remember what those were.

All I recall is that as I felt myself starting to lose it, I was finishing up a little booklet of meditations I'd written, copying and collating them with cardstock bindings to send to Kitty Davy at the Meher Spiritual Center in Myrtle Beach, South Carolina. It was touch-and-go whether I'd get them in the mail before my distress became a breakdown. I realized this during one of several walks back from the copy shop two blocks away from my parents' place, where I was living.

I did finish the job, getting the package of a couple of dozen booklets into the mailbox with the right postage. Kitty later wrote to thank me, saying she'd give them out to retreat pilgrims. It was a bit ironic that one of my pert little writings contained the sentence, "There's no place to fall but into the arms of God." Let's face it, God—your arms can be as soft as a Mother's, a bunny's, or a room-temperature stick of butter—and at other times, such as the one about to begin, as hard as pavement or wrought iron!

Walking away from the mailbox, I knew I needed to phone the hospital. Mother and Dad were out working, and when the doctor told me to come in, the only thing I could do was get into my car and drive myself there, even though I'd regressed into an almost catatonic state. I'm still not sure how I did it, stopping at all the red lights and making all the other split-second decisions and fine-motor acts entailed in a 10-mile drive across town.

2.

Well, this story isn't about that particular episode. I just mention it for instructive purposes, for there's a lot about the inner world of mental illness that you may not be aware of. Many times over the years, I was astounded when I discovered what *really* happened over the course of events—stuff you normally don't hear about or imagine. That's what's making me go to the trouble of telling you all this.

I had a new female friend who happened to hear me mention a song I'd written and asked if I'd play it for her some time. I went over to her place one afternoon and shared it, along with several others. She was moved, and gave me a big smile, which was dangerous, because I already found her quite attractive. Afterwards, I sat there in her living room talking with her while she, a single mom, worked in the adjoining kitchen making a salad for her kids' dinner. I kept seeing that big smile in my mind. Something in me began to get carried away with it, like a stallion running away from the calm corral of my usual thoughts. By the time I thanked her and left, that something was way out in the hills and still galloping, although I didn't say anything. The next day, though, I began leaving phone messages for her and writing notes, one of which I mailed. All of this was completely ungrounded, and within a day I received a reply—not from the object of my ruminations, but from the policeman husband of a mutual friend. At that point I realized that I was in orbit somewhere and could not get back. It was hospital time.

I checked myself into Jewish, a place which I learned (over several stays during the next couple of years) had great, although greasy, French-fried mushrooms in their cafeteria. This was my initial sojourn there. I settled in after the rather humiliating intake interview, in which you have to tell the admitting resident what "A stitch in time saves nine" means, and started to hang with the current crop of inmates. Most of them were insurance patients like me, and it was unclear what problems had brought them there. There was very little acting out in the ward, mostly just card-playing, scrabble, TV, movies, talk, and occupational therapy (OT). It was like we were all gathered at a friendly spa.

I still remember the rather distinctive clique that developed during that stay. A couple named Adrian and Sandy had somehow gotten admitted together and were the patients of a venerable female Dean of Psychiatry, whom I never even set eyes on. Adrian was an older fellow, a printer by trade. I can still feel his gentleness as I write this. Sandy was something of a Christian fundamentalist, whom I picture earnestly saying, "And I do believe these are the Last Days…"

Then there was Roger, a tall, freckled redhead with a face that resembled a wooden puppet's, and his very attractive girlfriend, Chantille. My impression is that they really were on a lark, that with insurance the hospital was cheaper than a bed-and-breakfast would have been. And there was Clifford, an intelligent African-American fellow who had a lot of business ideas and was always hitting the rest of us up for money. I also remember an American lady named Betty, whose distinction was being the first native American I'd ever met who had converted to mainstream Islam, and Dolly, whose mother later founded an upscale day center that became an oasis in the lives of the area's chronic mental patients.

After a few days during which I don't remember getting any care ar all, I received an order that I'd be getting a series of ECT. It turned out these were not at all unusual at Jewish. When I shared the news with them, both Betty and Dolly told me they were also receiving treatments.

3.

I had no idea what to expect. Was there a medieval torture dungeon in the hospital basement? I consented to the treatments because, although I was capable of sitting and playing cards with my fellow inmates, my mind was still whizzing away from me and there didn't seem any other way to get it back.

Over the next few days, I learned the ritual of ECT. Those of us scheduled for treatments on a given day were roused before dawn and led to a large, pastel-colored room with several adjustable reclining chairs. We were each helped into a chair, covered with a blanket, and left to wait.

When it was my turn, a nurse came first and explained the procedure. She told me I'd be receiving an injection that would put me to sleep for the duration of the electricity-induced convulsion. I'd experience no distress. When I woke up, it would be all over. She dabbed my skin with alcohol, attached the electrodes, and then gave me a rubber mouth guard similar to the one I'd worn as a high school football player.

A little later, someone came by to give me the injection, and the next thing I was aware of, indeed, was waking up and being led back to my room a little while later. After a bit more sleep there, I'd normally emerge for breakfast and whatever "the gang" was doing—OT, cards, or whatever else, unless I felt like reading or writing by myself. The treatments were scheduled for every other weekday, and the series consisted of five of them, I think.

4.

There was no drama whatsoever in the process. No one screamed. No one acted like a zombie. In a few days, remarkably, I felt like my old self again, minus a few short-term memories, which I was told would return before long. The horse was back in the corral. My thoughts were calm—normal.

I used some of my remaining hospital time to contemplate what I had experienced. How could this supposedly barbarous practice actually be so benign?

For a number of years I'd been a student of Eastern mysticism. During certain periods I'd had unusual—in a positive way—experiences. One of these involved experiencing God as Light. Of course, that is a mystical truism. God is spoken of as "brighter than a million suns and moons." I'd had only inklings of this, but even the inklings were very powerful.

However, I'd had a little revelation once that "God is Light" means *all* light—specifically, the streetlights along the St. Louis riverfront during a walk I took before dawn that day, and the light from the lamp in my room, deriving its radiance from the flow of electrons coming through the socket in the wall.

It stood to reason that if all light were divine, then the electric shocks that brought my mind back to its baseline were themselves a form of healing through Light, i.e. God!

I felt extremely pleased and satisfied to have arrived at this conviction. It did away with any sense of unnaturalness, any of those "medieval torture" caricatures. I felt myself laughing about the whole thing with a bunch of imagined—or perhaps merely disembodied—pot-bellied Zen masters!

5.

The side effect that I'd been warned about, short-term memory-loss, did occur temporarily, but actually turned out to be fun! I mean, if the spiritual ideal is living in the present, what is more conducive than not being able to remember the past?

I was returned to a childlike state of wonder. One morning I signed myself out of the hospital for a walk in the Central West End, the adjoining neighborhood that was home to many of St. Louis' coffeehouses, pubs, art galleries and antique shops. I encountered every sight—a modest diner where I sometimes had breakfast, the hospital buildings in the distance, the touch of snow, the Christmas decorations, the stately homes on an adjoining private street—with fresh joy, free of any clouds of personal emotion.

A little later that same Sunday, my parents picked me up for lunch and a movie. We went to a restaurant in the neighborhood, then to what may have been the worst movie I've ever seen: the recently-released *Popeye*, with Robin Williams and Shelley Duvall. Ms. Duvall, of course, was a dead-ringer for Olive Oyl, and Williams was a perfect Popeye, but the movie was cartoonish enough to start with, and in my state, it was positively surreal!

Still, my mental state made me like a little child, and I absorbed like a sponge all the love my folks showered on me, without my usual resistance. The memory of that day remains most dear.

6.

It wasn't until the treatments were finished and I was discharged that I discovered a more serious side-effect. Gradually, I began to realize that although ECT had slowed my mind, it had also closed my heart! Prior to the episode that had led to my checking into the hospital, I'd been living a life inspired by Love— by an embodiment of Love named Meher Baba, who had lived a perfect life of Love on Earth between 1894 and 1969. Our age, I'd learned, at first intellectually and then experientially, was an "Avataric Age." Spiritual opportunities abounded, that under normal worldly conditions were far beyond the reach of all but a few. My heart had opened numerous times to joy, even bliss. My life had become an adventure that awed and humbled me. There seemed no limit to possibility.

I had also experienced several "falls from Grace." Each was an indescribable agony. Following these, it could take months or a year to regain the poise and joy that had been so effortless that I had taken them practically for granted.

Now, back out of the hospital, I was ostensibly normal again. But as I went about my life, I came to realize that the spigot of Love—with a capital L—had been shut off. I really couldn't feel anything at all. I wasn't obsessed with anyone or anything: just completely high and dry.

I had nowhere near the expertise in "the technology of the sacred" to know what to do; nor did the psychiatrists I knew. I'd had one doctor during one of these dry periods, to whom I would often complain, "My heart is dead!" or not quite as dramatically, "My heart is closed!" Each time, he looked baffled and quizzically replied, "Your *physical* heart?"

As so often happened, I was thrown back on my own resources, which basically consisted of one thing: desperate, sincere prayer.

Part Two

1.

Several weeks after my discharge, I was trying to live a normal life, in spite of my non-stop internal suffering. I can't remember how I spent my days, as several periods during these tumultuous years have become blended within my memory. I don't think I had a steady job, but I may have been doing temp work here and there.

For a little diversion, I called my friend Ron one day and asked if he'd like to try a new little Greek diner that had opened up in the building that housed the Tivoli Theatre in the Delmar Loop. We decided to meet there at six.

Ron and I had both been born on February 9, 1948, though I'd been born in New York and he in St. Louis. We'd gone all the way through the public schools together. I still remember the two of us in kindergarten, building skyscrapers out of blocks with a few raucous companions, then dropping little female dolls down the center and thinking it was very funny! We'd both left the area after high school, both taken a spiritual turn, and by coincidence, were both back in our hometown. Ron had studied meditation and traveled to India twice.

The hot summer sun blazed at my back, even at 6 p.m., as I pulled the restaurant's door open. The air conditioning brought immediate relief. Ron came in a moment later. We sat down at a table toward the back of the small establishment and studied the menu. A little later we went up to the front window to order.

On the way, we passed the rather extensive, army-green back, topped by a mop of dirty yellow, of the only other customer in the place. As I passed, I noticed that the woman sitting there was around my age. Her table was full of crumpled napkins and what looked like scrawled pieces of note pager, and more spectacularly, a *huge* vertical pile of books standing a foot or two in front of her—twenty or thirty of them! Not wanting to stare, I didn't see any titles. But when the bell rang ten minutes later, and we returned to the window to pick up our moussaka and souvlaki and my Diet Coke, the mustachioed and authentically Greek-looking proprietor nodded toward her and hissed angrily under his breath, "She stay four hours and only buy coffee!"

This time, as I passed, I looked not at the somewhat disheveled table, but at the pile of books. They were all poetry or spiritual books! I noticed Yeats' *A Vision*, his mystical prose work about reincarnation and the phases of the moon, which I'd once tried, unsuccessfully, to read. She also had poetry by Emily Dickinson and Yevtushenko, a book about astral travel, and a volume of Krishnamurti. I was still only able to take in a few titles without seeming to gawk.

I went back and started eating with Ron, but for some reason my mind kept going back to the young woman and her books. I finally excused myself for a moment. I walked around and approached her table from the front (always go in the front door with people, a wise friend once told me). The picture I saw was still a little strange. She table's occupant was overweight, wearing an old army jacket, she looked as if she may have been up for two days. The table was strewn with straws and straw wrappers and pencils, in addition to what I'd noticed earlier.

"Excuse me," I said. "I couldn't help noticing your books. I write poetry and have spiritual interests, myself. Are you a poet?"

"I try," she said, revealing a really bad set of teeth. She simultaneously pointed to a small notebook in front of her, stained with coffee and pencil smudges, with messy cursive scrawls in what looked like verse form.

"I tried to read *A Vision* once, but it was too complicated for me," I said, not yet ready to hear her poems. "I like Yeats' poems, though, and I love the way he writes in his essays."

"He was a great one. I love that he practiced magic, as well as being a poet."

"Do you have a particular spiritual path you follow?" I asked.

"I'm in Eckankar."

"Astral travel?" I asked gingerly. "I've been taught to be a bit wary of that. Someone I know couldn't get back into his own body one time, because somebody else was in it!"

"It's not really just astral travel. We're taught that we're not the body. Astral travel is just one way of actually experiencing that."

"I see," I said. "Have you ever heard of Meher Baba?"

"Yes," she said. "Our teacher has quoted him. 'Love is self-communicative…'"

"Well, listen, my name is Martin," I told her. "I don't want to be rude to my friend over there, but I like talking to you. Maybe you and I could hang out together some time."

"Ok," she said. "You can show me your poetry, and I'll show you mine. Here's my phone number." She scribbled it on a piece of paper, and I picked it up. I said goodbye and started walking back toward my own table, wondering what had possessed me to approach her—while at the same time feeling I'd had no choice about it.

2.

I'm having trouble producing Gail for you, reader, pulling her out of a hat and making her real. I can't find her voice, beyond those little snippets above. It was all a long time ago, but what is time, where landmark events are concerned? Maybe I didn't listen to her as well as I should have.

I'll try to work around that. The main thing—and this may be giving away what gives the story its suspense—is that being with this overweight woman with bad teeth, who came out of nowhere in the way I just described and then disappeared into the night every bit as abruptly a couple of months later, very naturally did for me what medical science could not do or even understand—it gave me back my heart!

We weren't exactly a couple. It's hard to put a label on what we were. Companions, I guess. We just hung out together. I was still living at my parents'. Gail and I would get together and talk about poetry, or I'd tell her Baba stories. We never went out on a date or anything like that. We had no friends who ever joined us. It was just the two of us—our own little society. She would always be wearing the same drab olive army jacket, the same old pants and shirt. But what can I say? The relationship was my Fountain of Life.

I guess some people saw us as a couple. Harold, the owner of Baton Music in the Loop, where we'd sometimes walk, would stand outside his shop sometimes when there were no customers. He'd flash a big smile when we went by, brightly greeting us with, "Hi, Gail. Hi, Martin!" He knew me because I sometimes bought guitar strings and songbooks at the store. I'm not sure how he knew Gail's name. Behind his greetings, though, I felt Harold had us pigeonholed as two local eccentrics, people who had been defeated by life and had become "outsiders," like the bearded former professor and his sister who lived together in their car and sometimes walked those same streets. It's painful to acknowledge even now, but I guess there was at least a bit of truth to Harold's perception.

Gail and I didn't have sex, but we had a couple of brief, spontaneous hugging sessions. During one of these, I had an unusual kind of revelation that may have been the key to our connection. One evening, we were in my parents' living room—a beautiful long, golden space with a black marble fireplace. My mom had a flare for interior design.

We were lying on the carpet, looking at a book, and I gathered Gail up in my arms and just lay there with her, both of us feeling secure. We looked into each other's eyes. As we did so, I began to feel an atmosphere that became so powerful it all but displaced my sense of where we were physically.

In this atmosphere, we were somewhere and something I can only surmise we'd been in a past lifetime: two lepers, living in a dark cave, with only our bodies for warmth, only our two bodies clinging together. We had each other. That was all we had, our only relief from the vast loneliness and isolation of our lives as pariahs.

3.

I took Gail to a Meher Baba meeting because I was sure that, with her spiritual thirst evident in that tower of books at the Greek restaurant, she would soak up the Love there like a dry sponge. The St. Louis Baba group met in the home of Michael and Cynthia Shepard. A huge, powerful painting of Baba hung before us there in the living room. I was excited about bringing Gail. These gatherings and our little group had truly fed me since the Shepards had moved to St. Louis and began hosting them a couple of years before. I kept glancing across the room to where Gail was sitting, amid the mystical poems and songs, the readings of Baba's Messages, and one young lady's account of her recent pilgrimage to the Myrtle Beach center that Baba had visited three times, to see when my friend would "get it."

But she never did. In fact, midway through the meeting, Gail pulled out a book she'd brought, and began reading. Everyone was tolerant, but it seemed like kind of an antisocial thing to do. She was making a statement: "There's nothing here for me, so I'm just going to slip into a parallel universe." I had to accept that my assessment of things had simply been wrong.

4.

Sad that I was that I wasn't able to bring Gail the particular expression of Love that I felt was the gift of gifts, right before her, I was by this time back in the saddle of life, so to speak, due to the gift she had given *me*. My own life felt so natural that I scarcely thought about the past—the obsession that had brought me into the hospital, the shock treatments, or the terrible desert of dryness I'd found myself after they ended, with no trail out until I met Gail. Sometimes the openness and the love of life that had become my usual state again is best known by its absence, and by the relief and gratitude during those first precious days of return.

Toward the end of the summer, Gail called me one night and asked me to drive her to a psychiatric emergency room. I waited there for hours with her. She was having some kind of hallucination, but she wouldn't tell me anything about it.

They finally admitted her. When I went to visit her there a few days later, she told me she was being discharged the next day and was moving to live with her sister in Virginia. She had become uncommunicative and seemed paranoid, and I didn't even know why.

She departed on schedule without letting me visit to see her off, and leaving me neither address nor phone number. Had I unknowingly hurt or offended her? Or was the attitude she seemed to have toward me part of a wholesale withdrawal from life? I never found out.

Afterward, I walked around with only the memory of this unusual companion who had come into my life from nowhere like an angel summoned for a specific purpose, who disappeared without a trace when the purpose was fulfilled. Sometimes I think, "Well, maybe she really *was* an angel, or an *abdul*, one of the special agents God uses who can take any form."

5.

I went on to leave town myself within a year. I had recently read "The Wind of the Word," a poem by Francis Brabazon describing a dramatic encounter with God in the wilderness. It might sound tacky to say that I myself, shortly after, began encountering Spirit in a similar way right there in the city, blowing me this way and that in downtown St. Louis each night, after I had obeyed an intuition to rent a room there and look for a job. But I followed the wind, and that following bore happy fruit. A few nights later, the wind beckoned me across a Mississippi River bridge with my thumb extended. I ended up living near the Baba Center in Myrtle Beach, and spent an extraordinary year working for Lyn Ott, a former painter who had produced some 500 canvasses of Meher Baba and then gone blind due to a congenital condition. With difficulty, he had made the adjustment to being "a painter with words," and needed someone to help him with a novel he was writing. Following the wind brought me a year in heaven.

6.

The events in this story took place a long time ago. I'm more of a tree with roots today, quite the tumbleweed I was, but something recently got me thinking about the tumbleweed times and some truly extraordinary things that happened then. A literature professor once summarized for our class the theme of a certain novel, *Go Tell It on the Mountain* by James Baldwin, as "sometimes you have to go down to go up." That's just how it was several times, back then, and one of those times was that period after the shock treatments, when my heart was closed airtight and I had no road before me—until, as if by chance, I walked into a Greek restaurant one evening and found a young, offbeat woman with fifteen books piled up in a tower at her table.

All of this was a good twenty-five years ago, now. As someone sang once, and is still singing on jukeboxes and on YouTube—what a long, strange trip it's been.

The Life You Save May Be Your Own

1.

I'm sitting in my psychiatrist Dr. Cho's office in the basement of St. Vincent's Hospital, where the psych ward is. We're somewhere near Staten Island harbor. I don't know exactly what direction it's in, because I was pretty disoriented when Boris and Martin brought me in here a month ago. I couldn't speak.

I believe now that that was because I was choked with rage toward Boris. Amazing, to find oneself in such a bizarre state, unable to verbalize a single word! And not due to any physical cause, either.

Dr. Cho is behind his desk, waiting for me to say what it is I want. Our meeting's a bit unusual. Usually, we patients are at the beck and call of our doctors. That is, if we're not totally ignored, warehoused to pace the halls, go to OT, and gain weight on the carb-rich meals they serve here, until discharge. Yesterday, however, I requested to see my doctor.

"Yes, Mr. Markley?" says the doctor, his big square, bespectacled face surveying me.

"Dr. Cho, I was wondering whether the hospital makes referrals to halfway houses." I've been lying awake for hours every night, now that my discharge is imminent, scanning my mind for a solution to the problem that I have nowhere to go. I certainly won't go back to Boris', and I know very few other people in New York City. Nor do I feel strong enough, not to mention wealthy enough, to live alone.

"Why yes," he replies as matter-of-factly as if I'd asked him the capital of Colombia. "The hospital runs two halfway houses. If you like, I can look into them for you."

I'm dumbstruck. Flabbergasted. *"Then why the hell didn't you tell me?"* I want to shout. But I suppress my anger, compose myself and say very simply, "Yes sir, I would like that very much. Please do so, as soon as possible."

2.

It's two days later, just after breakfast. I walk out to the hospital van. The January air is frigid, and the shock of this cold contributes to my sense of having been reborn from a closed-in, stuffy womb. It's my first time outdoors in a month. The view across the harbor to Manhattan is spectacular, but the view in any direction through the sweet outdoor air—sweet even with its admixture of New York smog—is delicious, like seeing for the first time.

We drive about a mile, mostly down streets I don't know, before the driver pulls up and lets me out in front of a large, blue-grey residence with white shutters. I walk up steep cement steps built into a hilly front yard. On the slab of front porch, a few rocking chairs seem to bask frigidly.

I ring the bell. In a minute, a face that looks like a Groucho Marx mask appears in the little window. The door opens and a flabby man, still looking quite Grouch-ish, greets me. "I'm Harvey, the assistant director," he says. "You must be Martin. Ronnie, our director, is waiting upstairs to meet you. Follow me, please."

Harvey leads me up two flights of stairs. Before we get to the second, enclosed one, I glimpse a rather formal living room, full of plastic-covered sofas and "pretty" landscapes on the wall. I can see through an open door to a dining room/kitchen with a couple of long tables. The hums of both the fridge and the heater bring a throbbing life to the house.

I also notice the quiet residential corridor on the first floor, and an identical one on the second.

"Everyone here goes to a day program from 9 until 3 on weekdays," Harvey explains as he walks ahead of me. "That's why the house is so quiet now. The only ones here are you, me, Ronnie and one resident who is home sick."

Ronnie is waiting in a little crow's nest office in the attic whose walls are lined with full bookcases. He rises and comes forward to shake my hand as I appear in the doorway. Harvey, having delivered me safely, returns back down the stairs.

"So why are you interested in living here?" Ronnie asks me after our introductions.

"My family's in Missouri," I say. "And the person I was staying with before my breakdown is part of the reason I ended up in the hospital."

"I see," he replies. "Well, let me tell you a little about Wendover House. Residents are allowed to stay here at for up to six months, and after that, if they choose, they can move on to a supervised apartment. Everyone here is required to go to a day program on weekdays from 9 to 3."

"Harvey mentioned that," I say. "I'm willing."

"Good," Ronnie says. He pauses to look at me a moment and then continues. "We have a vacancy. If you still want to move in after I give you the tour, you're welcome to do so."

We go downstairs and he shows me the house I passed through a little while ago. He takes me into a bedroom. It has two cushy twin beds, a desk, dressers, more landscapes on the wall. It appears a lot more comfortable than my freshman college dorm room was.

The tour ends in the kitchen.

"Still want to come?"

"Definitely," I say. "It's clean here. I feel a sense of order."

I don't mention this, but during the past hour I've felt the first presentiment in a long time that there may be a way forward for me in life. Since I came to New York a few months back to take a series of "human potential seminars," which quickly morphed into confrontational nightmares, nothing's gone right. Fleeing to Boris' big house on the hill—I should've heeded my premonition when I heard someone refer to it as "Toad Hall"—I found my old friend now believed himself some kind of guru and exerted a complex, crazy-making spell on me. To avoid him, I began spending my days in fast food restaurants, shopping centers and libraries in far-flung locations on the island, retreating into a literary world. I attempted to save myself by reading and writing in notebooks, where I could still think my own thoughts.

But this "medicine" hadn't been enough. On an otherwise indistinguishable, grey day, I'd snapped. Since then I'd felt drowned in a dark whirlpool, until this past hour. This halfway house introduced the possibility of a safe environment. Here, I intuited, I might be able to begin to get my feet back on the ground.

"Well, good," Ronnie said. "We'll expect you the day after tomorrow."

"One minor question," I say. "I'm trying to place your accent."

"Israeli," Ronnie says.

The last thing I do before leaving the house is to ask to use the phone to call my mother, collect. There, in that humming kitchen, I share this latest development. She, who'd laid some serious "issues" on me during my childhood, has lately been my phone buddy, standing by me during the whole crisis, and I want her to know the good news.

3.

We're all at the dinner table at Wendover House. I've been here two months now. Barbara, the twenty year old with the little-girl pigtails who could be pretty if she didn't have the crazy look in her eyes, is down at the end of the table acting out again, babbling loudly enough to make everyone in the room uncomfortable: "He touched me, I said no but he did it anyway, I'll cut his dick off, I'll use a kitchen knife, I can do it! This food is shit, tastes like shit, shell pasta again? I love my brother, I need him, I can't live without him, I want to marry him, then I'll be safe, I..."

"Barbara!" Marty, the counselor, interrupts her sternly. "You need to stop. Stop now! Or else go to your room." Barbara lowers her voice to a whisper. I can still hear, but now it's an indistinct murmur, possible to ignore.

On my right, tall, thin Robert, with his thick black bangs and perennial smile, is talking, to me, I think, about Lou Reed, whom he idolizes. Robert has Walkman headphones on his ears, as usual. "You should hear this damn album! This guy is outrageous! He gets the 7th Avenue subway in the song! He actually went in there and recorded it, like the damn thing's an instrument in his band!" Robert is likeable and good-natured, but his conversation is limited. I get the feeling he may have lost some brain cells during his druggie phase.

Mario, across from me, is wolfing down his pasta quietly. He gets up to get seconds. Or thirds. Another seemingly cheerful guy, he has kind of a grey complexion. Probably medicated. Most of the residents are, I think. Mario's around 30. I try to guess what's wrong with him. Like Robert, he seems too simple, too innocent for a person his age in the late 1980s. Whimsically, I picture him as a young man from a mafia family, traumatized by witnessing too many murders.

They never tell you what's wrong with anybody here. Lots of elephants in the room when we gather. The only one I've really heard diagnose himself is Irv, the thin, morose 40 year old with whom I have more common interests than anyone else, even a mutual acquaintance. He's a very sensitive person, whose terror about what will become of him when his 90-year-old parents die has caused him to withdraw from life.

I pull myself away from the table and go downstairs. We're supposed to socialize after dinner, down here in the TV room. Socializing: the panacea for every mental illness. Sullen Bill is sitting on the sofa watching a movie on Comedy Central. He glares at me and I can almost smell him burning. Had James Dean not already come and gone, had Holden Caulfield not already been written, Bill could've blazed those trails. Something intense happened to him, too, but I don't dare ask.

I hear more tromping on the stairs. Laura's thick legs appear; then her face confirms her identity. Laura, the overweight girl whom I can tell has also come through some terrible trauma, yet another one who seems heavily medicated. She always has a smile for me, though. And she's literate, shows me the poetry she writes.

Following her down, with deliberately heavy clomping, is my roommate Chris, a young man with a red crew cut who's *so* late-adolescent he could play Wally in a remake of *Leave it to Beaver*. He's still another "nice guy" about whose condition I don't have a clue.

The others, as they finish eating, join us one or two at a time. Now Mario and Chris and Robert are having a belching contest and arm-wrestling over in a corner. Bill has turned the TV all the way up so he can hear. Barbara's babbling again, standing up next to the sofa in her T-shirt that shows Mickey Mouse propositioning Minnie with "Yo Baby, Yo Baby, Yo Baby, Yo!" A counselor's even helping Julia, 85 years old and almost totally preoccupied with just standing, sitting, or walking, to get down the stairs.

I have to get out of here.

4.

The day program has turned out to be, in its own way, as stifling as the house. At first I had hopes about it, too. Bill and I are the only ones from the house who go to this "elite" program for people who supposedly have the intellectual capacity for a full recovery and re-entry into society. The first morning, he was asked to show me the bus route. You have to transfer at Victory Boulevard, so it's slightly complicated. We were together about half an hour. He just stared straight ahead, though, even when we were waiting for the bus.

The program is in another big grey residence. The whole thing's a little weird. There are only seven of us, just six until recently when Scott, a 20 year-old who's quickly gotten kind of thick with Bill, came. We take up all the time of two professional therapists and an art therapist who comes twice a week. Someone's indeed pouring a lot of resources our way.

I was eager to go at my healing until Nancy, the director, with her short, spiky haircut, cut me off the first time I started talking about a real issue in group. Nancy just stopped me in the middle of a sentence. OK, so I should maybe have known that she'd want to protect the virgin ears of pretty Marilee from my soliloquy about my compulsive masturbation—how it's always followed by an agonizing period of energy depletion that can last two or three days. Marileed was the only real looker in the house, just a year or two out of high school. The first day, I asked, "Were you a cheerleader?" "No—a Twirlah," she answered in her thick New York brogue. Belinda, our other female member, is an African-American about 30, nice but heavily drugged.

Even worse than my interrupted monologue was what happened last week. I'd been feeling incredibly jealous of Bill with Marilee. They've become best buds and always disappear together at lunchtime. It's hurt my male pride. I felt I had to bring that up in group, too, my feeling of exclusion, or day program would become too painful to endure.

Even though Nancy looked like she wanted to kill me when she saw where I was going, and Marilee, asked by Nancy if she minded the topic, answered with an exaggerated smile, "Not if you keep it sho-at and sweet"—and even though nothing really changed as a result of my breaking once more the taboo against discussing things up close and personal, I somehow felt less squelched after getting everything out in the open. But Nancy's renewed glare sort of snuffed out any remaining hope I'd had of the day program ever being any real help. After that, I took it as a place-holder, the necessary price of the roof over my head.

By the way, the next day back at the house, Bill pulled me aside and, talking to me for once, gave me his lowdown about both our prospects with girls like Marilee: "The reality is," he said, "Is that these chicks are all gettin' screwed by cops and businessmen. We don't have a chance!"

My whole sense of "path" that had emerged that first day at Wendover House is in danger, after these two months. In fact it's practically gone, drowned under floods of chaos and sham. I feel pretty much back to square one. Lord knows how far this tailspin may go…if I don't do something. But what can I do? Like those nights during my hospitalization, ticking the thoughts sleeplessly away at an apparently insoluble problem, I don't have a clue.

5.

Exploring the island on the bus last Saturday, I passed an art supplies store in a neighborhood I'd never been in before. On a sudden whim I got off at the next stop, walked back there, and came out with a bag full of materials: a thick pad of 18x24" watercolor paper; both watercolor and acrylic paints; an assortment of brushes; and a round metal palette with little cups. It was just a hunch. When I got back to the house, I pushed the bag way under my bed and wondered if I'd ever use it.

Now as I slip away yet again from the noisy basement, the bag of art stuff comes to mind. I ascend the stairs. It's very quiet up on the main floors of the house. I go up the next flight, down to Chris' and my room, and enter. Chris is still down doing his nightly belching with Sal and Robert, thank God, and I bathe in the refreshing silence.

I reach under my bed and pull out the bag. In a couple of minutes, I've retrieved an old newspaper down in the living room, and put together a little set-up in the middle of our carpeted floor. It looks curiously shrine-like. The big pad is open to the top blank sheet, a blizzard of white. The little palette-cup is filled with primary colors and white and black, the way my old teacher at the university taught me. Brushes and a cup of water sit there too. Now I pull the pillow off my bed and sit down on it with my legs crossed.

What am I supposed to do now? I'm a "recovering mental patient" at one of the low points of my life. I've had creative experiences before. In college I did an independent study, drawing and painting mandalas. I've written stories; written and done illustrations for children's stories; written songs. In fact, wonder, and expressing it, has been my ticket through life since early adulthood. But now is now. I've been a basket case for months.

I try to meditate, staring into the white page as if wanting it to tell me something. It doesn't. I concentrate some more, and I'm not sure if it's intuitively or merely impulsively that I pick up a medium-sized brush, dip into the red paint, and make a blotch in the center of the page. The mark isn't big, but it's exceedingly bright, contrasting with the white expanse.

The red and the white seem to interact, and I feel a force field. Or is it my imagination? I decide to accept the irrational, that the color, the field are indeed "guiding" me, telling me where to put the next blotch. It takes a different shape. Soon, I'm mixing an earthy brown in another palette-cup, dabbing the page with that color. I start making staccato marks, modifying the mix periodically with more yellow or red. I still have no idea where I'm going. I pull myself back for a moment and look at what's accumulated on the page. Suddenly, I flash: it looks like a map, some kind of abstract map. Needs a boundary. I pick up a calligraphy brush and create a large black circle.

Three hours later, I look down again at what's emerged. In the center of the page is a stylized mandala. At its hub is a radiant sun. Inside the black circumference, city buildings face inward, converging upon that sun.

Outside the circle, the abstract pattern still resembles some kind of map…"the suburbs"? Beyond that, towards the four corners of the page, are simple wilderness images: hill, desert, mountain, forest. A brilliant lapis sky unites them.

I've been hypnotized by my own creation as it worked its way out from somewhere inside me, until it attained this "objective" existence on a page. As I gaze at it now, I'm pulled in strongly by the center sun. Then I feel myself radiating outward. I marvel at the piece, and at what just happened: my dissolving into a process of creation, which has resulted in this work of art that no one will ever duplicate. The funny thing is, when I come back to myself, I have to think to remember, "I'm a mental patient in a halfway house." I don't feel anything wrong inside me! If this experience tonight wasn't a fluke, then it's not me that's off; it's the surroundings I've fallen into, the past six months or so. As I continue to bask in feelings of joy and accomplishment, I begin to plan an immediate future of similar nightly experiments.

I realize that I'll have to patiently put up with all my external circumstances. I'm in no position to even think of anything beyond them, until I know more.

6.

Every night for the past two weeks I've slipped to my room, prepared my materials like a ritual magician, and ended up after several hours gazing upon a new world that's emerged on a page from inside me. Almost more startling, each of these worlds seems distinct. Where do they all come from? One night's painting expresses nostalgia for childhood. It shows a boy looking into a world of his imagination, depicted as a fancy paddlewheel steamboat sailing down a river like the Mississippi I grew up near. Another night, it's a pair of huge, outspread hands containing fields, orchards, mountains, sun and sky. Still another night produces an ancient, white-haired man with wisdom in his eyes, overlooking a sleeping youthful figure.

I don't even fully understand all the images, but I feel their power. This daily experience of being an archetypal "ferryman," bringing original images from unconscious realms and fixing them in form—in this case, paint—so that others can share them, is making me a more confident person. The creative reservoir has proven itself not to be fickle. It's indeed been there whenever I've sought it. Of course, I'm humble and grateful. I literally felt like nothing, very recently. It's literally redeemed me.

7.

The real challenge continues to be not the "art time," but rather making it through the uninspired rounds of the day without antagonizing Nancy or Ronnie until, in the night hours I re-enter my inner sanctum and access once again the life-giving magic. But I've been doing that passably well, I think.

Tonight, I've just finished the daily ritual of preparing the setting with the afore-mentioned priestly sense. I'm sitting on my pillow in that breathless moment, poised to pick up a brush, when there's a knock on the door. Chris wouldn't knock, so I'm puzzled.

"Just a second," I call, and rise carefully, walking to the door and opening it a foot. Ronnie is standing there, and now I see the warrior, whom I've heard taught weaponry in the Israeli army, in the way his face is set.

"It's been brought to my attention, Mr. Markley, that you are spending too much time alone," he begins sternly. "You are isolating from the others. This will not help your recovery. You are required to socialize. I think you know..."

It surges up from so deep inside me there's no more censoring it than there is censoring a volcano. I positively erupt with righteous anger: *"Who, just who, do you think you are?"* I open the door wide, moving away from it toward the room's center. Ronnie comes in and stands a few feet away. "Who do you think you are to presume you know so well what I need?" I demand. He has the power to put me out on the street. But I know if I back down, all is lost.

"I am *not* isolating," I continue. "I am *painting*! Who *said* that endless socializing and rubbing shoulders with a roomful of disturbed people will produce some miracle of healing?" I pause, then continue. "Do *you* say that? Drop your damn textbook! You know as well as I do that it will *not*!"

I can't help my tone. These words are *escaping* from me. They're not an act of will from my personality. They come from some deeper place.

But that's no guarantee he'll listen. I *like* my housemates, but I simply refuse to acquiesce and waste my entire life "mingling."

I show Ronnie the work from my cardboard portfolio: the child-nostalgia, the symbolic map, the wise old man, the whole array. I know he can assert his authority. One day a few weeks ago, he somehow got the idea that I wanted to have sex with Barbara, and he warned me in no uncertain terms.

But now, suddenly, he looks like a big child. I've never seen him this way. The warrior appears completely disarmed. His swords have been beaten into plowshares. His eyes are clear.

"I understand what you're saying," he says quietly, after looking again at me and the paintings I'm still holding up. After another brief pause for looking, he adds, "Yes, you know, I think you're right. Please forgive me for disturbing you."

"I do," I say, still in shock from his turnabout.

Ronnie quietly backs his way out of the room, smiles at me, and pulls the door shut in a quiet, respectful way. I breathe deeply for a few minutes. Then I begin to paint.

8.

It's early July. I'm about to move out of this place next week, to an 11th floor apartment in a high-rise, with a single roommate, the next stage in the system. Frankly, though, I'm starting to think I may have had enough of the system.

In the present moment, however, while I'm still here at Wendover House, I'm making good use of the place. I'm standing in the under-used living room where 13 of my paintings, matted and framed, are sitting on the floor, leaning against the front wall. In my hands I'm holding the last, bending down the metal clips on the back of the frame. This one is a colorful portrait of a sultry-looking lady I sketched as she dawdled at the ferry terminal one afternoon. Ronnie, who now displays on his office wall a color-Xerox I gave him of Manhattan's skyline nestled within the petals of a lotus flower, has given his blessing to my using the room as a staging area.

"Hey, I hope I'm not late!" a voice bellows in from the hallway. Scott, from the day program, has volunteered to drive the paintings over to the AMB Gallery in Hoboken, where they're going to be hung as part of a four-artist show.

"No, Scott, perfect timing," I reply. "You want to go up and get Bill?" I was stunned when my former antagonist, sullen Bill, was so impressed with the portfolio I showed him a month or so ago that he didn't have a snide or even a clever retort. He just kept nodding as I pulled up paintings, and when I finished, said only "wow."

After the initial "miracle painting", which in the show bears the title, "City/Self Mandala," the finished pieces started to pile up, an average of one a night for more than a month. The pile was getting messy, so one Saturday I took the ferry and subway over to Pearl Art in Chinatown and bought the portfolio to keep them safely in. When that too was getting filled, I called an artist friend to ask if he'd take a look. We met at a pub in the Village and he, too, nodded and nodded. When he'd gone through everything, he said, "You know, Cory Julian has opened an art gallery over in Hoboken. Amy Wilkinson is the manager. I think she might like these enough to show some of them."

I got permission to go to Hoboken after day program one day, missing dinner at the house—ferry to Manhattan, then a train from the PATH Terminal under the World Trade Towers. Hoboken was in the process of major gentrification. I found the gallery on the main street. Amy too had nodded as she perused my portfolio, and when she'd finished, told me about the group show coming up and invited me to join. She stipulated that everything had to be properly matted and framed, and that it would cost me a couple hundred bucks to do that. I made another trip to Pearl in Chinatown and ended up choosing silver metal frames with mats that would complement the individual pieces. I did all the framing and matting myself, right here.

As I place the last finished picture with the others, I hear running on the stairs. Tall, thin Scott, a little puppy-doggish in a nice way, and behind him Bill, bulldog-like as usual, enter the room. Bill appears entranced when he sees the paintings all dressed up for display. After a long gaze, he says, "Man, you've really accomplished something!"

I step back and try to look through his eyes at the array of bold color and playful, imaginative form. That Bill, with his wounded, sensitive temperament, has risen out of his own secret preoccupations to say what he just said leaves me feeling a success even before getting to the gallery. Of course, it was the experience of creating these works from nothing that connected with the living spirit within me and brought me back from the dead. But it helps, it really helps, when others confirm the value I feel in my work. What else is there for a human being to want than such bridges to hearts and minds? I can only wish something similar for Bill.

Whatever happens at the gallery, and wherever I end up living when I leave here, I feel I'm walking now on pretty solid ground. I've found my purpose, the thing I'm alive to do. I've registered for classes at the New York Art Students League in Manhattan, and will begin the daily commute as soon as I'm free of the restrictions the house imposes. But in a way, that's secondary. I discovered the gift within. Wherever I exercise it, that's where it will remain.

Bill and Scott begin lifting and carrying the paintings, cradling them delicately as they would little babies, down to Scott's old station wagon. I carefully pile up several more and carry them down the steps, joining my two friends. One more trip and the loading is complete.

It's a sunny day. I look back at Wendover House, remembering the winter day when I first walked up those steps, that day when a fragile path seemed to open. And now, another journey is beginning.

Adieu, Rivendell

Part One

Flight under cover of darkness

I walk out of my house at 4 a.m., carrying my duffel bag and guitar, and make sure the door locks behind me. The neighborhood is dreaming, deep in a clear summer night. The nearby streetlight reflects brightly off the top of my Nissan in the driveway.

Stashing my two objects in the trunk, I shut it, open the driver's side door, and strap myself in. In a moment, the engine breaks the neighborhood's early morning silence and I pull away, turning right at the corner. A few short blocks later I turn left onto Highway 17, the main north-south thoroughfare of the Myrtle Beach area. Its lanes, too, are deserted this early. A mile south, passing a green wooden gate on the left, I lift one hand off the wheel and put it to my heart. I turn my head briefly in the gate's direction while going by.

I try not to think too much about what I'm doing. Ostensibly on my way to St. Louis to visit my parents for a two-week vacation, I've pretty much decided not to return to Myrtle Beach.

This is a very big thing, for I've longed to live in the community near the Meher Baba Center for most of my adult life. The Center is a 500-acre spiritual retreat and wildlife preserve right on the Atlantic Ocean. Meher Baba, regarded by his devotees, including me, as the Avatar of our age—the equivalent of Buddha or Jesus—visited there from India three times during the 1950s.

I'd been enchanted by the Center's spiritual atmosphere since first setting foot on the land 25 years ago. For the past two years, I've lived in my own house a mile away and two short blocks from the ocean, which my folks bought for me when they came to feel I was settling down in life. For the four and a half years prior to that, I rented a room in a friend's trailer. I volunteer at the Center in different capacities several times a week, always feeling it a privilege. I also give a once-a-month concert in the library, occasionally recite poetry or sing in the Meeting Hall, and feel especially proud that my paintings were once exhibited there.

It's my personal life that's a mess. Supposedly a "celibate aspirant," I just don't know if I can take the loneliness anymore. Things are all knotted up, and I've found myself in a process of deciding it might be best to make a new start elsewhere. Much of this process has gone on without conscious volition.

I often reflect on the seeming irony of my "revolving-door" relationship with the Center. I never intended that. A permanent resident of this community of "Baba-Lovers" is what I'd always wanted to be. Each of my several moves to the area over the years was accompanied by the thought, "This is it." Then, after awhile, something would happen and I'd end up living a couple of hundred or even 1,000 miles away, with no immediate prospect of coming back. I've come to think of this phenomenon as being "spun out."

This time, in my self-talk, I describe my plan as "leaving God to find God." In spite of what I feel were my best efforts over the years, I've spoiled this holy environment for myself. But if Baba—God—really is "everywhere and in everything," it has to be possible to discover Him anywhere! During the difficult recent months, I tried hard to "get His attention." In the Lagoon Cabin, where the God-Man gave interviews during his 1950s visits, I've lain prostrate before the Master's chair at discreet times when no one else was around. Perhaps the seeming lack of response occurred because Baba *knew* I needed to leave!

My belongings will have to stay back in the house for the time being, as I'm finding it impossible to deal consciously with either the shame of leaving or the practical matters involved. Instead, I'm keeping myself in a sort of conscious state of denial, allowing the plan to remain in the back of my mind.

At 48th Street, I cut over a quarter of a mile to the bypass, and just west of downtown turn right onto state highway 501. Through a series of state roads, I'll link up with I-95 at Florence, 60 or so miles away, and in a day and a half or so, driving mostly on interstates, I'll be in St. Louis.

It feels good to be on the road. For a day or two, there are no decisions to make. I don't live anywhere. I'm just a person driving. CDs and books on tape will help pass the time.

Heaven, then purgatory

Memories begin to visit me as I drive. My first trip to the Center took place a few days after Divine Love began pouring out of a photo of Meher Baba in a friend's advertising office in Chicago. I'd been in the city visiting former college comrades. A day or two after that experience, another member of our old group, someone who'd also "come to Baba," told me about Kitty Davy, Baba's longtime disciple who helped manage the Center until she passed away in 1991. "She's *on fire!*" he said. The fire in his voice prompted me to query the friend in whose office the experience had taken place, about whether I might be able to visit there. "Ask and you shall receive" seemed to be the order of the day. Though I had been thinking in terms of taking a Greyhound to the Center, my friend offered to take a few days off from his job and drive me, along with two other people new to Baba.

We drove all night, though the car was buffeted by storm after storm all through Kentucky, Tennessee and North Carolina. I imagined the storms as "seven seals"—and who knew? Everything seemed to have mystical significance during those days.

One of the female passengers and I had clashed several times while in the close quarters of the car. However, upon arrival at the Center, we went for a walk together and ended up holding hands. As we walked, she told me she felt the presence of Angels, and that they seemed to mass near the fence that divided the Center from the surrounding land.

Uncannily, Meher Center was a colony of people who seemed in essence just like me! It was almost too wonderful! Somehow, it brought to my mind the last scene of *Fahrenheit 451*, in which a small group has migrated to the woods. Each person has memorized a great book, because there are no more printed books in the world. Their little community is really the last bastion of values in the world, and each cohort walks around reciting his or her entrusted work aloud to keep the memory strong.

I first moved to the area five years after that initial visit. Again, there were extraordinary experiences, but it was as if I had no traction. In a month, in spite of my intentions, I was gone.

Five more years after that, I'd lived a heavenly year in the community, working for Lyn Ott, an artist who had done hundreds of "expressionist" paintings of Meher Baba. Lyn had had a progressive eye disease, and had finally lost the last of his sight. Amid the anguish of losing this "most precious possession," he'd slowly made the adjustment to being a painter with words. He'd authored a book about his development as an artist, which had culminated in his meeting Baba in India in 1967 and deciding thereafter to paint Baba in every canvas. Now, he was working on a novel about the Dutch artist Jan Vermeer. One day, in the Center's kitchen, he asked me to help with the project by reading back new chapters, noting edits that he made as I read, making my own suggestions, and finally, retyping each section.

Adieu, Rivendell

During that year, I'd frequently contributed music and poems at the Center's meeting hall. I'd felt not only inspired, but useful. I'd had a *role*. It seemed likely that through Lyn's sponsorship, invisible forces had granted me this sense of feeling grounded and at home at the Center and in the community.

Near the beginning of our association, I'd asked Lyn for a few days' leave. Feeling the need for a female companion, I'd thumbed down to Florida to try to find my former wife and convince her to come back with me. Arriving in Cocoa Beach, where friends had said she was living, I spent a warm winter day sunning myself beside the Atlantic, with no idea how to go about finding her. Rising in late afternoon and walking over to the main street, I asked the first person I saw, a young man riding past on a bicycle, "Do you know where Eleanor Beardsley lives?" The young man pointed to a house almost right in front of us and said, "She lives right there!" I smiled, but that's the way things happen with Baba sometimes.

Eleanor and I had sat in the front yard and had a heart-to-heart talk, at the end of which she'd affectionately declined my invitation. Then, on the way back, I met a young lady at a Howard Johnson's counter just off the highway. During our conversation, she said, "Yesterday, in New Jersey, I got on my knees and asked God for a better life." We travelled together by bus for several days, through Daytona and Savannah, finally arriving in Myrtle Beach, where we started a life together. Some months later, at Lyn's suggestion, we'd married. It seemed that Baba was giving me everything I needed so that I could do my work undistracted.

That whole year, the movies of Meher Baba shown on weekends in the meeting hall were *not movies*! Baba's image was on a screen, yes, *but as real as flesh*! Love flowed! Words fail to convey the experience. I sat at Baba's feet, as close to the screen as possible, and tried to surreptitiously touch my head, or a hand that had touched my forehead, to the floor as often as possible.

The most recent six and a half years of my life, though, had been different. Arriving at my friend Ed's trailer after driving down from New Jersey, I could hear the strains of my favorite spiritual anthem, "Victory Unto Thee," playing on a tape deck inside. It seemed like Baba's welcome, a presentiment of good things. But all this time later, I felt myself drying up on the vine. Efforts to find a compatible girlfriend had ended pathetically. My blunders had left me feeling like I'd burned bridges. My initial resolution to endure the loneliness had begun to change, as I found myself involuntarily withdrawing from people. Even during my weekly stint as the Center's night watchman, a position I'd loved, I began to avoid Center guests. Recognition seemed to be dawning that I lacked some sort of *ripeness* that permanent residents of the community must require.

Change of plans

Nearing I-95, I pull into a McDonald's for a drink. Taking out a map and studying it while sipping a soda, I notice that I-95 does not meet up with any direct route to St. Louis, as I'd previously believed. It connects to I-40, but today's I-40 is not the Highway 40—also known as the Express Highway—that had carved its way through St. Louis during my childhood. That thoroughfare has since changed its name to I-64, and runs much farther north.

A better route will be to head north on the state roads and go west upon reaching I-64 or I-70. State highways will be more scenic, and I'm not in the mood to rush for another reason, as well. Tomorrow is July 10, Silence Day. It's the anniversary of Baba's refraining from speech for spiritual purposes, which began in 1925 and continued through the last 44 years of his life. Devotees around the world observe silence on that day every year. For me, it will be better to be on the road than at the home of my parents, where such unconventional behavior might lead to endless note-writing.

Part Two

The visit that was not a visit

Three days later, at 9 a.m., I pull up in front of my parents' place, totally worn out from driving all night. I grab my things from the back seat of my car and straggle up the walk to the lobby of the three-storey building. A moment after I push my folks' button, a loud buzzer sounds. As I pull the handle of the glass door, the white door of their unit halfway down the hall cracks open. Mother comes out and peers in my direction. She waves and smiles as I walk towards her. She's known my arrival to be imminent, since I phoned during breakfast over in Illinois, just in view of the St. Louis skyline. Reaching her, I bend slightly to give her the obligatory, yet affectionate kiss on her wrinkled cheek, not far from her expensive, natural-looking reddish-brown wig.

"You must be exhausted!" she says. "Put your things in your room and come sit down for a minute or two before you go to sleep."

A little while later, I'm sitting opposite her on the sofa, marveling as I always do at her flair for combining the antique and modern in her decorating. "You do look tired," Mother says. "Why didn't you stop at a motel?"

"I just wanted to get here," I explain. "Those extra two days in the mountains while the car was being repaired were nice, but once it was ready, I didn't want to dawdle. After dinner last night—at the Colonel Sanders Original Restaurant and Museum, by the way, which I happened to pass in a little Kentucky town—I just felt like making a dash! Listening to my book helped keep me alert. I pulled over at rest areas twice and napped. Anyways, I'm here and I'm safe. By the way, where's Dad?"

"He's at the zoo, doing his docent work. He'll be back by the time you get up. I hope you can have a nice vacation here. Think about what you want to do together. We'll take you to Bevo Mill for dinner one night. Maybe we can go to the new casino one afternoon, too."

"I don't know if I want to go to a casino, but Bevo Mill sounds like fun," I reply. "I remember that place, down on the south side; on Gravois, right?"

A wave of exhaustion passes through me. "Ok, I guess I'd better go to bed now, you're right." I rise and kiss her on the cheek again before departing down the corridor that leads to the guest room.

The secret's out

I enjoy much of the next couple of weeks, as I enjoy most of my visits to St. Louis. Revisiting a hometown allows a person to inhabit old haunts, free of knotty associations they may once have had. It's a delicious life in a purely aesthetic realm.

And yet, although thinking of my stay as a visit affords me some relief from the pressure about where I'll live, another longtime challenge pursues me even in St. Louis. My paintings were discovered by a gallery owner in Myrtle Beach a few years back, and her sponsoring of my work helped it to become somewhat popular. Tired of day jobs as a clerk or substitute teacher, I'd seen a possible road to becoming a professional artist and writer. I'd been highly enthused when a recording engineer friend had helped me create an audiocassette of my short stories, adding a literary "product" to the art sales.

The marketing of the tape, however, had been a dismal failure. Still nursing deep disappointment, I feel a need to produce a whole new body of work. Influenced by readings in Jungian psychology, I believe that the artistic exploration of "complexes" and the archetypes behind them can release and transform energy and lead a person forward in life. Every morning after breakfast, I write. At the very least, I write "morning pages," the daily free-writing exercise that Julia Cameron recommends in her book *The Artist's Way*. Every afternoon I go back to my room, carefully cover my work area with newspaper, and paint until "something" emerges.

When I'm not pursuing this quest directly, I work out at the JCCA gym, visit the few friends who still live locally, or, occasionally, go for a drive or hike in the country. Most days I rendezvous with the folks at dinnertime. Time passes very quickly.

Our dinner at Bevo Mill is meant as an end-of-visit treat. The venerable German restaurant is in a hundred-year-old windmill that Anheuser Busch himself used to dine at during his buggy drives from his country estate to the Busch brewery. The walls are covered with 19th-century paintings and the waitresses dress as Bavarian *frauleins*. The food is excellent, although the atmosphere is rather stuffy, with clientele consisting entirely of elderly Caucasians.

On the way home, I sit in the backseat as Dad drives the air-conditioned car through the dark city. I feel protected, like a little boy. I realize, though, that it's time to shatter that illusion. Delaying the sharing of my plans is no longer an option.

Mother says, "So you'll be here a couple more days, then? Have you reconsidered about the casino?"

"I don't think I'll be going back to Myrtle Beach," I blurt out.

"What?" she asks, with surprise.

"I don't want to go back to Myrtle Beach. I think I'm going to stay here."

"But you've always wanted to live near the Baba Center!" she says. "Don't you like your house there?"

"The house is fine," I reply. "I just don't feel I really fit into the community. I want to try living here." I know my parents will not be able to make me return to Myrtle Beach. Since I was a little boy, they've scarcely been able to make me do anything.

"Well," Mom says, always one to divert intensity by postponing it, "You can stay with us awhile longer and think about it. I suppose if you decide you really don't want to go back, we can call that friend of yours who sold us the house and have her put it back on the market." Mother sounds tired, but her voice is gentler, more accepting, than I'd expected. None of us talk much the rest of the way. When we arrive at their building, Dad parks in the garage and we all go up to bed.

In the morning, I go out for breakfast as usual. Something is different, though; I can feel it. My status has changed. I'm a resident now, not a guest.

A change in the weather

Within the week, I begin to have run-ins with both parents. Mostly, these are about seemingly trivial matters that clearly represent archetypes whose vast power lies under the surface. Mother predictably quibbles about my hair, clothes, room and diet, and especially whether I exercise enough.

An incident that took place during a particularly inspired period I'd gone through years before suddenly comes to mind. She and I had been standing in the kitchen across from one another. I'd been trying to share with her a sense of the Divine Beauty of existence, and she suddenly interrupted me with the words, "You have a spot on your forehead!" She went on to repeat them as if the matter was a grave emergency. Finally, I went into the bathroom to look in the mirror. Noticing a miniscule dot of white, possibly a tiny piece of dried white-out, I sighed and peeled it off.

Now, she's even more set in her ways. The two of us are like the warm fronts and cold fronts that give rise to the tornadoes I remember from growing up in this region. "Just visiting" had been one thing, with everyone on their best behavior. Some lever has been tripped, and every little incident now ends up as a flash point!

With Dad, too, a memory from years before surfaces. I'd come back defeated from my first stay on the West Coast, feeling totally lost again only a year after my Meher Baba rebirth experience. Upon my return, the habitat of my upbringing seemed unmasked, somehow. Words of love spoken there now had to vie with the experience I'd had of what I knew to be the real thing in its purest form. During this period, the sight of my father caused me to go into a rage. Something had felt wrong with the family picture. After a few days of these outbursts, however, Mother had nipped them in the bud by spiriting me off to live with her brother and sister-in-law in Cincinnati.

Now, Dad's an old man. He still goes to the office for a couple of hours a day, but mostly he watches TV or goes out to a movie or restaurant with his brother-in-law Nick and his old friend Harold, both retired and declining physically. Though Dad is quite obese, his favorite activity is stopping at the neighborhood Burger King for snacks.

His car was recently rear-ended and he got bruises. It was nothing really serious, but he's made an insurance claim that reads like a brazen attempt to cash in: "This accident has ruined my Golden Years," he stated in his report. I can't help but comment, "Dad, that letter is shameless!"

Mom hears my comment and comes into the kitchen, inserting herself between us. "You leave him alone!" she says sternly. "Your father has a bad heart. Do you want to kill him?"

"Of course not," I say. "But did he have to pad his claim that way?" Over on his chair, Dad looks innocent, as if he doesn't understand a word that is being said.

"He can do whatever he wants at this point in his life! Leave him alone or leave this house! Do you understand? And while you're at it, why don't you go and clean off the paint you've gotten on the furniture in your room!" Her emotional upset appears to be turning her white. I've only seen this happen once before—but then again, I've been living away for years.

"Now I'm hyperventilating!" she continues amid labored breathing. "You see what you've done? Now I have to go to the emergency room!"

"Just take it easy," I say.

"It's too late for that! You leave him alone while I'm gone!" Mother flies around the condo like a fluttering bird, grabbing her purse and slamming the door behind her. Dad and I are alone. We go into the bedroom peacefully to watch *Seinfeld* together, but I'm beginning to realize that my mother has entrusted herself with the responsibility of protecting both of their lives, and everything else comes second now.

She gets back two hours later, still huffing and only a little less pale. They're so frail now, I realize sadly. I really might inadvertently kill one of them.

It's time to move out.

New home at The Cambridge

On a visit to the city of several months' duration a few years before, an old friend had told me about an inexpensive rooming house in the Central West End, a section of St. Louis filled with coffeehouses, pubs and antique stores. The place had been only slightly run-down, and rather charming. I'd enjoyed my stay in the humble quarters.

The morning after Mother's trip to the emergency room, I phone the manager of the old building, known as The Cambridge, and make an appointment. Harold, the owner, remembers me, and has his son show me a third-floor unit with a view of the street through the branches of a great sycamore tree. The garret is furnished with a rollaway bed and a desk-sized table, chair, lamp and dresser. Its little kitchen has everything anyone could need, all crammed into a tiny alcove. The place is perfect!

I pay the deposit and first month's rent and go back to get my belongings at the folks'. When I announce the move-out, they wish me well in a calm, friendly manner. We're already back on good terms. Trying to live with them had been solely responsible for the crisis.

Once at the Cambridge, I realize it's time to accept another hard truth. My effort to be a full-time artist and writer, at this point in time, is a wash and possibly even a delusion. I'm still painting and writing every day, and the images from my brush, in particular, seem powerful. Yet I feel like I'm running on a treadmill—spinning my wheels. My explorations don't seem to be leading to any deeper integration.

There can be only one reason for this: it's not the right time. Baba is saying, "Let it go." I need to go out and get a job.

This insight comes as a great relief.

The right job

I buy a St. Louis Post-Dispatch and open it to the classified ads. During my extended visit a few years back, I worked part-time as a delivery courier. It hadn't been a UPS-style company with a uniform, a company truck, and a constant deadline rush. With the small companies, all you have to do is fit the dispatch radio onto the console of your car, slap a magnetic company logo on its side, and stick an antenna, also magnetic, up on the roof. There are deadlines, of course, but reasonable ones.

I set up an interview with First Preference, a small company in the warehouse district of University City, where I grew up. The young, friendly human resources director seems happy to see me. He sends me right out for training with an affable, bearded fellow named Tom. I sign on for three days a week, still wanting to leave myself some down time, in case the muse starts visiting again.

The day after training, I set out on what quickly becomes an adventure of discovery. My formative years were largely confined to the suburbs and to Forest Park, where the zoo and art museum are. A year spent driving a taxi in my '20s served as a profound education, but it turns out there are still areas of the region I don't know.

A couple of mornings a week, I and a number of other drivers are called to a warehouse near the company office. At the far end of a mid-sized earthen parking lot, a rolling door by the loading dock yawns open. Dozens of brightly-colored plastic tubs lie stacked in the storage area. These contain pharmaceuticals to be delivered to drugstores all over the metropolitan area. Many of the stores are located in small towns across the Mississippi River in Illinois.

As the weeks go on, I come to love filling my car with the tubs, setting off across the river on the interstate and then leaving it to follow state highways that wind through cornfields and woods. Finally, I arrive on the outskirts of a town, and a few blocks later I'm cruising down the main street. These towns retain an early 20th-century charm, with marvelous Victorian homes, old churches, and quaint commercial zones. Some of them are county seats and have large public courthouses with ornate stone statues out in front. Many shops in most of the downtown areas are closed, however, having met their demise when Wal-Mart opened on the outskirts.

I easily meet most of my delivery deadlines, but in a lot of ways, being a courier is, as my taxi stint was, as much an education as a job. I get to know the foothills of the Ozark Mountains to the southwest and the towns along the Mississippi to the southeast. Over in Illinois, I often make deliveries to the old steel mills in Granite City, which I don't remember having even passing during my childhood, and to the oil refinery farther north in Wood River. I cross both the Missouri and Mississippi rivers to make runs to Alton, a small city built on hills sloping down to a dam and canal lock, behind which the Mississippi is like a lovely lake.

In the central part of the city of St. Louis, I find myself delivering wiring, light bulbs, toilet paper or any number of other things to ancient factories with bricks almost black with soot. These are the ones that are still functioning, though the city has been losing both industry and population for years.

These plants make ball bearings or other esoteric creations that become components of products or machines. Their large buildings, constructed in the 1920s or earlier, when the city was among America's largest and fastest-growing, often have mullioned windows with dozens of panes. Rubble is strewn everywhere in the yards, and many objects indoors are covered with grease.

Getting out of my car, I shout near the entrance of a building. Receiving no answer, I walk into the front room. Finding no one there, either, I enter a winding maze of dark, tunnel-like passages that lead through cavernous rooms full of complex, roaring machinery, with wheels moving and gears meshing, but betraying no clue about what's being made. Sooner or later I find someone able to sign—usually an old fellow in grease-spattered overalls, who looks as if he came with the building!

When autumn arrives, so different from fall in the South where I've been living for years, the leaves become almost supernaturally beautiful in their shades of gold, red, yellow and orange. In some places, they're exclusively a pale gold, making it easy for me to imagine I'm in one of J.R.R. Tolkien's elfin lands. All this, and then when my first pay check comes, I feel like leaping in the air! I assumed the job would pay a pittance, and have been doing it largely to make a point with myself. However, the check for the first two weeks is enough to cover rent, food, and gas for the whole month. I feel rich! Except for medical insurance, which my parents insist on carrying for me, I'm earning my keep.

On my rounds, I tune into NPR first thing each morning to get the feel of the day. A little later, I switch to my current book on tape. In this way, I keep company as I drive with Mark Twain, James Baldwin, Aldous Huxley, Dostoyevsky, J.D. Salinger, and many other souls who were or are, in Henry James' words that I'm fond of, "people on whom nothing is lost." I always carry a notebook in the car, and write journal entries during delivery lulls. Though I've written a great deal of verse in my life, that muse, inundated by recent events, went into hiding awhile back and still hasn't resurfaced.

A life assessment

The great leafy sycamore branches brushing against the window in my little bohemian garret leave me feeling that I live in a tree house. Sometimes the moon shines brightly through the branches, and I imagine "making tea for this friend who has come to visit." I enjoy romanticizing my loneliness this way.

    A person looking at my life might think I'm happy, I realize one day. Philosophically, I believe that happiness is always with us. Looking back, even at hard times, years later, a person can find it. But in truth, my present is still often a funk of loneliness, accompanied by a sense of sexual need and frustration. The procession of attractive and enticingly-clad women that I see in public leaves me semi-aroused much of the time. When the pressure becomes too much, I masturbate. However, that kind of relief exacts a price. Since my late 30s, this act has been followed by a sense of severe depletion that can last for several days. During such a period, my thinking is weak and I lack the energy to connect with other people.

    Nonetheless, I continue to make what feels like a heroic effort to face life, which wears a new but similar face every day. Surely Baba is pleased with the steps I've taken.

    Though things are better than they were, I've noticed that, since coming to St. Louis, I'm not really able to feel my feet touching the ground. There must be additional steps to take. Someday, hopefully, I'll experience myself standing squarely and solidly upon the Earth once more.

Part Three

Cyber-launch

I arrived in St. Louis in mid-July and had moved into The Cambridge by the first week of August. A week after that, I began my courier rounds. Summer passed on to Indian summer and I found myself in the midst of almost neutral, golden days on which the sun shone brightly but without heat.

The plunge into winter weather comes in early December. I wake one morning to an inch of snow. The Cambridge looks like a fresh white maze, nearly unrecognizable. Going out on its byzantine walkways and fire escapes to empty the trash, my eyes open to purity, peace and silence. The world seems to have been freshly saved.

My loneliness continues, however, punctuated by a few more wondrous snowstorms and a few memorable books on my car's tape player: *Cry the Beloved Country*, which I'd read but not read when it was assigned in high school; Salinger's *Franny and Zooey*; and some masterful short stories by William Faulkner.

My 50th birthday, in early February, draws near. My parents, back to being my biggest fans, invite me out to lunch. My birthday is a workday, but I arrange to sign off at noon, stash the radio, antenna and company logo in the trunk, and drive to their condo. Mom had asked where I wanted to go, and I'd mentioned a new Brazilian place. I've passed it on deliveries, way down on the south side near the river, where the city always smells like hops from the Budweiser brewery.

The restaurant turns out to be closed on Mondays, and we drive up to the new Planet Hollywood in the cobblestoned Laclede's Landing area between downtown and the river. Sitting with my folks in the huge, tacky dining room, I start feeling sorry for myself. Even at 50, I'm still a kind of "boy-man" with no life outside the people who brought me into the world. I'm thankful for their company, though. Without it, I'd be *completely* alone.

After lunch, they present me with my birthday gift: my first personal computer. Until now, I've only had occasional connection with the World Wide Web. A friend in Myrtle Beach had shown me his setup once. I'd been impressed, although it had been hard for me to understand what I was seeing on something called AOL. Then, just before leaving town, I'd shown one of my taxi passengers some greeting cards that the art gallery had made from my paintings. "Wow, I could set you up on the Web, and people all over the world would buy them!" the young man had said. I'd given him a set of cards and my phone number and then had waited expectantly. But no call had come in the next few days, and after that I was gone.

After lunch, I drop the folks off at their place with hugs and thanks, and drive back to The Cambridge. In two trips, I carry the PC, monitor, and accoutrements up to my room. Still a little tipsy from the beer I'd had at the restaurant, I flop into bed for a nap. When I wake, it's getting dark. I take a walk up to the pizza-slice place on Euclid Avenue, then come back and begin puzzling out, manual in hand, how to set up the computer.

A mere hour later, thrilled to see the words "Welcome" appear on the sky-blue screen, I begin unpacking the various programs, starting with Outlook Express, the email application. I send my first email. It's to my cousin Shari, the only person whose address I have, greeting her and thanking her for picking out my computer in a two-for-one sale at a store near her home. Its twin went to her mother.

Eager to discover the sites on which a person can put art cards up for sale, and to join "Baba-Talk," the Meher Baba-related discussion group my Myrtle Beach friend had showed me that day, I search around unsuccessfully for another hour before deciding to call it a night. There'll be another whole day to look before my delivery gig resumes on Wednesday.

Finding the way

It takes two more days to locate and get on "Baba-Talk," because for some reason, searches tend to bring up old lists of topics or people, rather than the actual "How to Join" instructions. In that time, I've become a member of an online poetry group and a dream interpretation group. Anything you can think of seems to be out there! I've sent photos of my paintings, via the scanner that's part of the "3-in-1" printer I picked up at Office Max, to a website that indeed sounds eager to market them. My cousin has recommended that I enroll in a general PC-know-how course at the community college, as well as a computer graphics course she's taken, and I've done all that, too.

On "Baba-Talk," I finally reunite with old friends and begin making new ones. It's good to have a kind of extended spiritual family. Soon I begin posting anecdotes from work, book and movie reviews, jokes, and, as the muse has recently begun to stir once more, an occasional poem. I take part in the discussions, and in doing so, learn some of the downsides of the Internet One person can hog the attention of a group, and a friendly discussion can quickly turn volatile because people are so strongly attached to their views.

I now have an additional project to pursue on days off. The art card website's owners have stipulated that before they'll give me space on their site, I need to have an inventory: 50 cards of each of a dozen images. They have to be in shrink-wrapped sets that include envelopes, and ready to mail. I begin canvassing small digital print shops, and soon find one to do the job.

The new poems are what excite me most. Life is becoming unpredictable again—that means I'm living in the present! The muse who had fallen asleep is now insisting on being heard from time to time, and her voice, as often as not, is a zany one!

I sign a petition one morning on the Clayton Post Office steps, the aim of which is to ban cockfighting in Missouri. Walking away afterward, I pull out a notebook and write down a rant that turns into a poem I call "My Noble Act." The local NPR station had recently aired an interview with a farmer who raises fighting cocks for a living. "Ah loves mah birds," he'd said. My poem is about lifestyles made obsolete by new technology or changing public mores. It goes on to ask, "Are poems my cocks? / I raise 'em, / send 'em out / to fight (for recognition) / 'Ah loves mah poems,' I say."

By the time I finish, I'm giggling out loud.

Another spring

Nine months have passed since my return. The spring rains have begun. The feelings of intimate nurture that they engender are deeply precious to me.

One Saturday morning, sitting in the Starbucks a few blocks from The Cambridge as it pours outside, I flip through the pages of the *Riverfront Times*, the local alternative weekly. A spontaneous question arises in my mind: How much would it cost to live in a luxury high-rise? There are several of them in the Central West End, averaging 20 stories or so. To live up high has long been a dream of mine, although a minor one. "Just for fun," as Dad would say, I find the Classified section and begin checking. "LIVE IN THE CLOUDS: Executive House, 19th floor studio, 4419 West Pine" catches my eye. At the bottom of the ad, it says: $40,000.

Forty thousand dollars? Is that a typo? To *own* the place? This little dream is not necessarily an idle one, I realize. My parents are people of some means. They've earned and invested steadily all their lives, and both drive Jaguars. In New York or California, such a place would run

$100,000 or more. Here in the Midwest, my parents can easily afford it as an investment and I, while living in town, can be the caretaker! Plus, I know Mother is a bit ashamed that her 50-year-old son lives in a "shabby rooming house."

Visiting for breakfast the next morning, I show them the ad. That's all it takes! Good motives, bad motives—$40,000 is not even serious money in these years of unprecedented economic boom.

A pretty blonde agent shows us the unit a few days later. It's beautiful and immaculate, with a parquet floor. Although it's a studio, someone has separated off a tiny bedroom area with a makeshift wall. There's a living room, a dining alcove and a kitchen. Everything about the place is right. Dad writes a lump sum check on the spot.

For furnishings, my mother takes me to an upscale consignment store. We find an exquisite abstract-expressionist carpet, a comfortable sofa and a glass dining room table. While the condo deal goes through, there'll be an unavoidable week or two of waiting. Soon, though, when I arrive at my place of residence, a uniformed doorman will let me in and I'll ride the rest of the way up to my home in an elevator.

A rainy spring night

On a rainy Monday night after dinner, I decide to walk over to the Executive House. It's a pleasant walk, with my umbrella over my head in the spring shower. Leaving the creaky Cambridge, I stroll up to the corner of Euclid and McPherson and then down Euclid, the main drag of the Central West End. The first block is brightly lit with shops, restaurants and pubs. After that, the street goes dark, and I know I'm passing the walled-off backyards of stately homes on several exclusive private blocks, including one where the poet T.S. Eliot was born. After two blocks, the street brightens again with more shops, pubs and restaurants.

There isn't really a rational reason for this walk, except that anticipation of the move has me a little jazzed, and I love walking in the rain. I splosh in little puddles on the sidewalk as my thoughts—the endless meditation—go on: a person is always the meat in a sandwich, I muse. You can't see the piece of bread ahead of you, the future. The one behind, however, the past, is visible as memory. In spite of recent efforts and improvements, my memories still leave me feeling lost. Is there something wrong with my wiring, my judgment? I've had new starts in life, slate wiped clean, more than once, by great spiritual beings and forces. I'm more fortunate in this respect than most. But from one perspective, life is very long, as my fellow St. Louisan Eliot wrote in one of his poems. Within a year or several, even new, fresh pages seem to become submerged in tangles of karma and imperfect responses to challenges.

I quickly go over the past six years. Ever since my first visit, I've identified the Baba Center as a real-life version of Rivendell, the Elven citadel in *The Lord of the Rings,* a spiritual fortress in a fallen world. During one stay, I looked out over Long Lake and could see Meher Baba's face in every lily pad. That hadn't been *my* doing, but pure and simple Grace. That Grace had seemed natural at the Center. It made sense that if a being of infinite consciousness had walked its paths and sat in its cabins a mere couple of decades ago, then indeed, anything could happen there for many years into the future.

Now, having tangled Rivendell up in the apron strings of my own shortcomings, I've "left God to find God." I have to keep believing that—as has been concretely demonstrated in my life many times, I keep reminding myself—all things are constantly being made new by the God-Man, and all things are possible *everywhere.* If I continue to put one foot ahead of the other and do my best, this wilderness, too, will surely yield to a connection with something or someone that knows my name.

Surely Baba appreciates my recent efforts to face reality, but more steps lie ahead. I don't really think of the move to a new living space up in the sky as a step. It's more of a horizontal motion. Yet even it will change my daily habits, the people I pass, the view from my window.

I cross Maryland Avenue and walk toward Lindell, the city's major east-west boulevard, lined with luxury apartment buildings. I turn left there and right again a block farther east, at Taylor. As I continue south on Taylor toward the next street, West Pine, the brightly spotlighted upper floors of the Executive House come into view. By the time I reach Taylor and West Pine, I can see the entire structure rising like a 22-storey cake lit with numerous candles! The thought that I'll be living there in two weeks boggles my mind.

I continue down West Pine until I stand directly across the street from the illumined edifice. There's no point in crossing the street and going closer still. I'm already face-to-face with my future—with a part, at least, of "the other slice of bread."

In Myrtle Beach, a house did not make the difference, and it's not likely to here, either. Material circumstances don't determine the quality of life. That depends on being in harmony with the One behind the many. This, in turn, depends on choices made in the face of karma.

I stand there, umbrella propped up under an arm, and fold my hands to my heart. *"Beloved Baba,"* I murmur. *"Help me to do better. Help me to live Your Life of Love all the time. All things are possible by Your Grace."* I recite the three main prayers Meher Baba gave to the world: the "Master's Prayer," the "Prayer of Repentance," and the short one known as the "Beloved God Prayer."

After that, I turn around and walk back up to the corner of McPherson and West Pine, stopping briefly to gaze for one more moment at the glowing building and its lovely reflection on the wet pavement. I turn again and this time, in the still-refreshing rain, continue back to The Cambridge without stopping.

Vertical motion

Naturally, in my new digs, it's a thrill to wake to the sun rising over the downtown buildings to the east, the park-like suburbs to the west, and even a little sliver of the river if you look way to the south. The fun of being up here is like a little kid's fun. This thing of fulfilling wishes, there's nothing wrong with it—you have to live somewhere.

But there's still no relief from loneliness. In the neighborhood post office one afternoon, I notice a particularly attractive woman in tight jeans and a denim jacket, and even "relieving the tension" at home doesn't get her out of my mind. A few days later, pulling into the gated parking lot at the Executive House after work, another realization arrives: I need therapy. Recalling that I've heard Catholic Family Services provides psychotherapy on a sliding scale, I phone them. No more fortune-charging, parentally hired psychiatrists. I'm an adult and I can manage things my own way.

The very next day I drive out to a pretty, gold-domed building on a wooded piece of land in a quiet suburban area. The place is a seminary for priests, but the Archdiocese has apparently decided it's also a good place for CFS. I sit in the office and fill out the required form. Turning it in, I get out a book. Before long, a short, bald and bespectacled man comes out and calls my name. I raise a hand and wave in response, then put the book back in my shoulder bag and follow him down a corridor.

"Martin, it's nice to meet you," the man says when we're seated in his office. "My name is Jerry. What led you to phone us?" He has a caring voice. I spend the session telling him how and why I've returned to St. Louis, what I've done for myself here, and in which areas I continue to feel stuck.

As we begin the next session, he asks about my history. I take him back to what I think of as "the fall" in my life, which occurred when I was about seven years old. I describe the glance I received from Mother as I tried on a new pair of blue jeans she'd left in my room. I try to convey to Jerry the desire I'd seen in her eyes as she spied on me from the hall through the cracked doorway. I'd only been able to see her because, as I admired myself in the full-length mirror on the door that led to my parents' room, the other door behind me had creaked slightly. That led me to notice her eyes in the mirror.

The whole thing had only lasted a few seconds. She probably just looked in the door, which didn't shut properly because its metal tongue was broken, to see if I was done, and then briefly got caught up in what she saw. Afterward, though, I felt as if I'd been burned up. I was too ashamed to even go downstairs to dinner later, until Dad came and got me. How would I ever be able to live in my body for the rest of my life?

Twenty more years passed in shame before my prayers for someone to trust enough to tell all my secrets to, were answered. On the day that someone appeared, the gate of my dungeon, which I'd believed to be locked forever, had swung open. My imprisonment, begun during childhood, had continued all the way through adolescence and into young adulthood, behind the masks I'd learned to wear for much of my daily life.

Jerry

Jerry is quietly supportive. He seems to empathize as I describe, in our next few sessions, a pattern of being strongly attracted to a woman while feeling the stakes too high to risk rejection by reaching out. I share how this emotional paralysis has woven me in knots on several occasions, and once led me, at least indirectly, to kick a policeman in the shin and spend some time in jail—though fortunately, and again, I believe, by some kind of grace, I was saved from getting a criminal record.

Jerry wears a rapt, serious expression on his face as I speak. When I finish recounting, he says, "Well, Martin, it sounds to me as if you're suffering from post-traumatic stress syndrome. Do you know what that is?"

"I've heard of it, and read an article or two," I say. PTSS, also known as PTSD, is just coming into the common vernacular. "After I got out of jail, that time I kicked the policeman," I continue, "I stayed in bed all day, with my eyes closed, for over a year. My doctor said I was like a concentration camp survivor who'd been released but had never recovered."

"Some may be left over from your childhood, too," Jerry says. "Even though you were able to share your secrets, having spent your formative years holding all that inside is likely still affecting you. We'll go easy, one little step at a time. I think you could use the Personal Ads to find dates. I think it's important for you, and I think you're ready now. The people who place Personals, many of them, are a lot like you. Do you think you might want to give it a try?"

An ocean of women

I dive into Personal Ads dating, which does, indeed, seem to be made for me. You're not so on-the-spot as with picking up the phone and calling someone cold. You have your ad out there doing the initial work for you, telling others what you're like, and you can peruse the ads of a seemingly unlimited number of available companions.

My first date is an attractive, vivacious 45-year-old who likes the outdoors. I pick her up and we drive over to Cahokia, a World Heritage Site across the Mississippi River. The Indian burial mound's flat, grassy top offers a panoramic view of downtown St. Louis. To reach it, you have to climb a steep flight of 120 wooden steps. The state-of-the-art museum across the road has beautiful sculpted metal doors. Tamara, my date, has lovely orange curls that shine in the sun.

The next week, we get together at her house to sing Frank Sinatra songs. "Old Blue Eyes" has recently died. I'd mentioned in my ad that I've bought the Frank Sinatra Songbook and would love to sing the songs with someone. I enjoy our session, and she tells me she does, too;

but after that, "it" happens. Tamara becomes impossible to reach. I leave voicemails and she doesn't call back. My weight had gone up during my self-pitying early days back in the Midwest. Does her disappearance have something to do with that?

But I, too, become scarce for some people who want to see me. Once, I arrive early at a restaurant and wait outside for my date. A little later, a beautiful woman who matches her physical description comes to the door. "Are you Doris?" I ask, but she shakes her head no. Still later, my actual date arrives, matching the same description but overweight (like me) and not attractive to me at all.

My family starts getting into the act. Dad's boss's wife has a single niece named Wendy, one of my favorite female names. It makes me think of a wind blowing through branches. Imagining what this Wendy might be like, I call and ask to take her to dinner. She turns out to be very unlike my wispy imaginings: attractive enough, but very worldly and definitely not my type.

My second cousin Sandy tells my Mom about a friend of hers with whom I might have something in common. This actually turns out to be true. Dining at a European-style restaurant, our conversation flows from the evening's start until its finish. We see each other several more times, but there's an unspoken caveat. She lives with a man—"a biker," Sandy says—who's away at drug rehab for a few months. It isn't clear that my new friend is really available. Furthermore, when I pick her up one day, she takes me on a tour of their ranch house. It has nice flowerbeds out in front, but indoors it's a different story. She and her partner own a large Airedale, and every room in the house smells strongly of dog or dog poop. I come away wondering how my friend can live that way!

Over the next several months I see blondes, redheads and brunettes— fat, thin, old and not-so-old women. It's a dating marathon, but nothing really sticks. It begins to appear that the ocean is not really so full of my species of fish, after all. The women I connect with more than superficially are few. Many of the people who use the Personals are indeed wishers who haven't been able to sustain relationships in their lives, and using the ads is their way of dreaming. On the other hand, I feel my own dreams in this realm beginning to run dry, as the same descriptions appear week after week. The devilish pattern continues: the ones you like don't like you, and the ones you're not interested in are chasing you. I start to feel like it'll go on and on, and I'll get old without ever finding anyone.

The muse

In other areas of my life, however, there continue to be hopeful signs. A certain momentum has developed: working at the job, seeing Jerry, and exploring online. I've added a once-a-week dance class that meets in a room at the library branch near the Executive House. It's taught by an inspiring student of Katherine Dunham, the modern dance pioneer who lives and works across the river in East St. Louis. My Tuesday and Thursday creativity days are never idle anymore. The dance class meets on Tuesday, and I also work on my art cards, which now need only to be shrink-wrapped in sets and sent to the website people.

The new poems keep coming! The most exciting one, "The Doormen," has been prompted by my conscience as it reacts to the institutionalized racism I note every evening as I'm buzzed into my new home by a uniformed person of color.

One morning, while delivering a package to an auto parts store in the city, I pen the beginning of a short story expressing both my loneliness and my hope. Noticing that the entire wooden counter where I sit waiting for a clerk to sign is carved with graffiti, I begin scrawling in my notebook. I imagine a character returning to a godless city after a spiritual pilgrimage in the East to a place like Meher Baba's tomb. The pilgrim brings a holy name back with him and repeats it silently as a mantra. One day, on an impulse, while waiting at a counter like the one

I'm sitting at, he carves the name into the wood. From then on he engages, unbeknownst to anyone else, in a "guerrilla mission" to carve and write the name, and keep repeating it silently, wherever he goes. In the months and years that follow, the entire city gradually blossoms in transformation.

God's name—according to great Masters, the most powerful spiritual force there is. I have "all my bets" on this. I remember reading in the *Ramayana*, the Indian epic, how Hanuman, the monkey god known as "the breath of Ram," crosses over from India to Sri Lanka on a bridge made of leaves with only the name of Ram inscribed upon them. When Hanuman himself is shown this miracle, the power of the simple name is too much for him, and both he and the leaf he is standing on sink into the water.

Sahavas

One Friday in early October, I take time off from my courier job. Someone has posted a notice on "Baba-Talk" about an Ozark *Sahavas* gathering, near Fayetteville in northern Arkansas. Baba used the word Sahavas to mean "intimate companionship with the Master." Nowadays, of course, the companionship with Baba is spiritual, not physical. Such yearly gatherings have sprung up in America since the '70s, and I've attended them in California, the Northeast, the Southeast, and near Chicago. This is the first one so "down home" for a St. Louisan, and I feel inspired to go.

It takes most of the day, driving southwest on I-44, to get there. After 250 miles I stop for lunch in Springfield, Missouri. Back in the car, I carefully follow the directions for leaving the interstate and picking my way through the fields and mountains of northern Arkansas. I've scarcely been to a gathering of Baba-lovers since leaving Myrtle Beach a year and three months before. A small group meets informally about once a month in St. Louis, but I haven't often felt up to going.

I pass the "Welcome" banner on a dirt road halfway up the side of a mountain. After parking in the long narrow clearing which is the designated lot, I carry my things up to the main cluster of tents. People are eating dinner at outdoor tables. I grab a plate and go through the line. Carrying my loaded plate towards the dining area, I'm greeted by several old friends, who invite me to join them. This kind of thing happens often at Sahavas gatherings. You never know who will show up. I agree to share a tent with Paul, an old apartment-mate from one of my early sojourns in Myrtle Beach.

Though the mountains are lovely and the Baba-lovers enthused, on Saturday I begin to feel a growing sense of separateness. I sing two songs at the campfire that night, but find myself envying several popular performers who are there. It begins to be clear, clearer than it's been lately in St. Louis, that I remain prone to depression.

I'm not able to do much more than go through the motions of participation on Sunday morning. Leaving for the drive home after the closing session, I feel that the bottom I've been slowly and painstakingly weaving in the basket of my world has fallen out. A stop at the small but excellent Springfield Art Museum on the way back, in a city that seems to have no downtown and an endless anti-abortion march going on along the closest thing to a main street, is the highlight of the return trip. In fact, I have to admit to myself that the museum's collection of 19th-century American paintings is the highlight of the whole weekend! As I drive for the next five hours under grey skies, I wonder, painfully, whether there's been any point to all my effort of the past year.

I get to St. Louis after dark and carry my stuff to the elevator, which hauls it up to my floor. I set my computer and monitor, which I'd taken along to make the gathering "the first online Sahavas," on the table, and my duffel bag and guitar case on the living room floor. Then I remove my clothes and climb straight into bed. Baba had said that deep sleep is a return to immersion in God's original oceanic bliss. That's definitely what I need right now.

Part Four

New day

I wake to sunshine, early enough to have breakfast and unpack before starting the day's deliveries. I reconnect the computer and monitor, an operation whose simplicity still surprises me, and make coffee while waiting for the machine to boot up. In a couple of minutes, I click the email icon. I see the "Baba-Talk" digest that comes every morning, and the companion one called "Baba," which features mostly quotes. There's the weather report and the Writer's Almanac, plus a poem that arrives daily and a few "spam" ads, which lately have been getting epidemic.

Then I notice a subject heading I'd missed. It says, *"Martin, you are a treasure."* My mind does a sort of double-take. Is it another ad, designed to get special attention? Who would write something like that? And why?

I click to open this one, as I had not done with the others, and read:

Jai Baba, Martin!

Do you remember me? We corresponded briefly mid-August re a mutual friend's health, after word appeared on the Listserv that he was in the hospital.

Well, I'm not popping on your screen to talk about him tonight. I want to talk about Martin. (God I'm being bold! Not like the polite intermediary who wrote you previously. Must be all the Wasabi I schmeared on my sushi tonight.)

Here's the deal: it all started when the newest installment of The Whim made its debut. When I got to the article, "Name-Dropping in the Baba Community," I began smiling, then wondering, then suspecting, then finally howling out loud by my open window around midnight. Your article definitely got my highest vote on The Whim's laugh meter! And so, what started out as a simple wish to write you and thank you for your wonderful humor became....

—The Martin Odyssey—

I said to myself, "Before you can write Martin, you must refresh your memory about his many talents. Get a snapshot of who this character really is." You know, like getting a corporate profile before calling the CEO. Except that I have nothing to sell.

So, what more exciting adventure could one have on a Friday night than to hunker down with the Listserv Archives and check out Martin!

You know, the next time you're depressed (if that sort of thing ever happens to you), check yourself out. It's quite a read!

The Odyssey began when I clicked on SEARCH. What was originally intended as a spot check to read a few posts soon became a tidal wave of laughter, fascination, curiosity... spilling over from Friday night into Saturday, and oozing into Sunday. I was hooked. Damn! Another addiction.

Did you know that you've posted 540 times since January 1st? And that's just on Baba-Talk! Let's see... 540 posts divided by 278 days... that's 1.94 posts per day. I know the frequency of your posts was sometimes sporadic. Nothing for a few days. Then one of your hysterical off-the-wall observational comments we all think but only you express. And written as if everyone on the List had just been talking about it.

As if what you were saying were somehow "normal." Or a movie review, written in the middle of the night, that no one ever acknowledged. Or a funny sign you saw from your car. The local weatherman who "caused" the weather. Karen Finley. Death. Always the first to offer a prayer and personal condolence. Hippo meat. Augustine of Hippo. Timing. Cyber-parades. Jokes. Screaming out in the cyber wilderness. Poetry. A publicly broadcast private giggle about what happened to strike you when you awoke. Or fell asleep. Storyteller extraordinaire. Canada. Tao. Book of the Dead. Sufi dancing. Family. Doubt. Fear. Highs. Lows. Unabashed self-disclosure. Talking-book inspirational message of the day. Lust. Obedience. More poetry. Empathy. Killer wit. Master of the unexpected. An irreverent tease. Quirky. Out there. Real.

    Always giving

    (Jeez, are these the newest 101 names of God? STOP!)

    but NEVER... dialectics, criticism, negativity.

    Martin, I suppose if I followed each person's thread through the Archives, I'd get a well-rounded idea of everyone. Yet I doubt any has contributed so fully from the heart and funny-bone as you have. You have been so generous with yourself. And I just want to say how much I appreciate what you've given.

    A while back, Emmett S. told me with great pleasure that your poems were now on the HeartMind poetry page, so of course I went there immediately. Re-read it tonight. Why didn't he announce you? I don't ever remember seeing anything about it. Did I miss something? There were some poems from the first half of the year (sorry I only got to early July... had to return to work today after the weekend odyssey) I thought would also be neat to have on HeartMind. You know, maybe with a touch of editing. Gems can get lost in the Archives, and people often rummage through the daily postings at breakneck speed. It's wonderful to take the time to stroll through and savor what's out there.

    And of course I visited your home page. Read your stories. Hey, maybe I'll even order a cassette! And looked at your artwork. You've been busy!

    I guess why I'm writing is because I feel I can identify with so much of your stuff. You've been like the Listserv's Everyman. You write reviews the way I speak about them to my friends. I have a girlfriend who told me years ago she'd rather hear me tell her about a movie than see it herself, because whenever she did go see it, she was always disappointed! I share your quirky sense of humor. And your whimsical observations: you take the smallest incident and automatically find relevance and current growth in it. Much pathos. And humor. Always humor.

No, Martin, this is not your memorial service, but your living appreciation service! I often regret that I never really learn about some friends until they're gone and their qualities and accomplishments are celebrated at their memorial. I always find myself thinking, "I wish I had known that about them while they were alive. What a full life they lived!" Consequently, I'm a real fan of sharing the goodies now. And letting folks know how appreciated they are.

Well, all this from someone who's never once posted on the Listserv ☺. That's just how I am. A one-to-one kind of person. Bold, yet private.

I send this to you now, so that the next time you're the only one awake and posting at 4 a.m., and no one's responded to your last 10 brilliant emails, and well, you're just bursting with frustrated creativity... you'll maybe remember that there is at least one silent one out there who appreciates your many gifts. And your willingness to share them.

You're okay Martin.

Jai Baba!

Bonnie

Effects of positive radiation

I sit, stunned, at my computer. I've long hoped that Baba has approved of my online communications. They are, in their way, attempts to connect not only with many, but with the One behind the many. If Baba has actually *enjoyed* them and decided to apprise me of that, the letter might be just like this one! It almost feels as if he wrote it through her.

Who is this person? I do recall an impersonal correspondence about a friend's condition, after I had publicly solicited information. Am I a "treasure"? Well, aren't we *all* treasures? We are *the* Treasure; the Soul. I smile, feeling the letter still warming me inside.

How does someone respond to a letter like this? Quickly, for one thing, I realize, for I have to get to work. I write a short note of appreciation promising more later, and click "Send." After putting on my jacket, I head out the door.

Snippets of the letter come to mind all morning. At lunchtime, I stop at a library on my route, read it again, and print out a copy. After work, I write Bonnie another short note. I realize my words have to be sincere, but also a bit cautious. Hers was not a *romantic* letter. I can't just fling open all the doors of my being, throw my defenses overboard, and express all my feelings, which include fond hopes.

I jokingly propose marriage, seeing humor as a good way to defuse pressure. Then I ask where she lives. The next morning, a new email from her says, "I'm a 30-year Sufi living in California." This leads to a bit of confusion at first—a 30-year-old? Twenty years younger than I? I feel, well, flattered, until the matter is cleared up by my asking whether she's the daughter of a long-ago acquaintance of mine with the same last name. She replies that he's a former husband. "Thirty-year Sufi" means she's been a member of Sufism Reoriented, the Sufi group Meher Baba chartered, for 30 years. The two of us are contemporaries.

We settle into a friendly correspondence—not every day, and not on any particular schedule, but steadily writing to one another about mutual acquaintances, people being obstinate on the list-serv, world events— anything. Life goes on, and remains difficult, with the single addition of this friendship.

Occasionally, I disappear for a day or two with no explanation. This happens when I'm going through one of my "depletion-and-recovery" periods and am too embarrassed to explain. Once, before Thanksgiving, I abscond for longer than usual. On the third day, Bonnie emails a request for me to call her, and appends a phone number.

I oblige, although with misgivings that turn out to be prescient. In my still-depleted state, I'm tongue-tied during the call. Afterward, I worry that this might injure or even destroy our friendship. The next day, I take a deep breath and write her the real reason for my absences.

Good morning, new skin

One morning, shortly after Thanksgiving, which I celebrate with my parents at cousin Sandy's, something is different from the moment my head comes up off the pillow. I can't put a finger on just what, and puzzle about it while getting dressed.

Walking outside to the parking lot under a clear December sky, to drive to the bagel place before starting work, it hits me: for the first time in several years, I feel genuinely glad to be alive. I'm *happy*! I'm not dragging myself around in a "fake it till you make it" mode. Every cell of my body feels at home, in effortless poise.

The change takes me quietly aback. At what time, during the previous night, did it happen? Driving to my first delivery pick-up, I celebrate while half-listening to *Morning Edition*, and some understanding begins to dawn. Bonnie has been pouring unconditional love and support into my being steadily for a month and a half. It's taken this long for the love to dissolve my shell. If I've had a tough day at work, or a contentious response or no response at all on the list-serv, she's been there every time with kind, consoling words.

I've had my own personal angel watering the roots of my being! Over the years I've affirmed to myself many times, "I am never alone," but overcoming the prodigious contrary evidence of my senses has often been impossible. Now I know I'm really *not* alone—*not* an isolated grain of sand in a great urban desert! I have a friend; a partner.

I drive on, out to Dorsett Road, which is a commercial boulevard in the county, for that first pick-up. The sky has clouded over by the time I get there. There's dirty snow, the last remnant of a storm a week ago, in the gutters. Telephone wires stretch above the road, between the world and the sky's grey. The buildings I see are concrete warehouses or haphazard small shops and box stores: what someone would ordinarily describe as ugly. Yet, all I see is glorious beauty. The collage of ugly-duckling elements now also includes the eyes of Love that have been newly re-awakened in me, enabling me to experience that it is all God's Original Light arriving and renewing Creation every second!

I still have Bonnie's phone number in my wallet. I have to tell her–to share the good news! I pull my car into the White Castle parking lot coming up on the right, and drive to the phone booth. Parking, I go in to get a cup of coffee, come back out, and dial her number.

"It's Martin!" I say, hearing the click. "I woke up *happy* today! I don't even know how to tell you *how* happy! The world is my little ball of silly putty! I'm in love with everything! And it's all because of you!"

The banks of old snow that have been plowed from the lot glisten in the sun. The silver and black of the phone booth shine like a vision, and the cup of steaming White Castle coffee I take a sip of is Divine Communion. No longer is Time the lord of the world. God, infinite God—that Love that first revealed itself to me nearly 30 years ago, and with which I've played hide-and-seek for so long—is *here*, naked, no longer eclipsed by grotesque shadows!

Here in the lot, lifting the cup to my lips again, connected with my beloved's spirit through the receiver, I can *feel* her heart responding to my words of gratitude! I drink once more to our new life.

APPENDIX:
Two Essays

My 45-Year Romance with Meher Baba

1.

I first encountered the name Meher Baba while walking to breakfast with an acquaintance at college in Sarasota, Florida in early February, 1969. The friend was carrying a newspaper, glancing at it as we quietly walked. Half way to the cafeteria, he said, "Here's an interesting article," and proceeded to read a brief story on the obituary page. The piece went something like:

> *"There was a man named Meher Baba, who lived in India and did not speak. He maintained for many years that he was God, and would break his silence before he died, and he died yesterday, January 31, 1969."*

My emotional response to those words was a kind of whimsical delight. That someone, somewhere in the modern world would *either* claim he was God, *or* maintain silence—let alone both, briefly lifted the quotidian veil, somehow. Before long, however, the name Meher Baba faded from my mind.

2.

The context for that "first hearing" described above was the cyclonic 1960s and its blast furnace of intensity, some of which I describe in the other stories and essays in this book. In spirit "the sixties" as a vortex of energy replete with new possibilities and some peril, lasted for me from spring of 1967 until sometime in the '80s.

In the late '60s, many of us were too young or immature to know the stakes. I was among those who played Russian roulette with chemicals that I really had no business messing with—although the possibility that LSD and other drugs ingested during my brief months of trying to "right myself" with what seemed their promise *may* have been a necessary tool God used to batter down my ego, whose defenses were particularly self-protective because of traumatic experiences in childhood.

Hearing Meher Baba's name coincided with my plunge into the psychedelic world and then my plunging again, eight times in all, to try to recoup my losses from the first time as well as to heal my life up till then. These plunges were into a deep pond which contained a Golden Key that I had lost. Each effort to recover it failed, although it sometimes appeared briefly that I was on the way to success. That turned out to be a mirage, as the story "Coming Into It" expresses.

The period also coincided with my 21st birthday, the coming of age alluded to in the title of that story—and with my expulsion from Sarasota's New College. Both events took place within two weeks of that memorable walk to breakfast.

My mother keened on the phone when I told her of my expulsion, like an Irishwoman who'd lost a fisherman son to the sea. I didn't feel consciously devastated, however. I felt I was moving *toward* something: a fellow New College student had offered the use of her family's land and farmhouse in upstate New York for an experimental community—a commune, as we called them. I felt this was my logical next step. Finally, away from meddling parents and university officials, I believed I could "create, 24 hours a day."

3.

I left New College in a drive-away car with several friends, on what was their—but no longer my—spring break. It was my first cross-country drive and my first time in California. It was all deliciously planned, this

Grand Tour, to circle back for a quick visit with my folks, followed by the move to the farm.

By far the most poignant irony I'd ever experienced was a growing awareness, as I neared our "utopia" waiting outside of Ithaca, that my mind was proportionately shutting down and refusing to cooperate. Psychedelics had brought up deeply buried emotions I had been defending against since childhood. I was raw. My mind, it seems, was doing for me what I could not or would not do for myself, removing me from this unbearable nakedness by shutting me down completely.

Instead of realizing utopian dreams in the six months I spent at the farm, I became "a living dead man." I tried to isolate from the other residents by putting a mattress down in the old milk room of the barn and making it "my room," leaving the farmhouse where everyone else lived. Finally, my parents came and begged me to come home. I vehemently refused. But one day not long after they left, I realized how deeply I was mired and that nothing would ever change if I stayed. I admitted defeat, caught a Greyhound, and became, for a year, my mother and father's child again.

4.

The condition of living in the family home was that I see a psychiatrist once a week. I believed my case was hopeless, that the drugs had done something to my brain that was beyond repair. However, there was nothing to lose by complying with the request, and in fact it bought a year frozen in time that I look back on with great tenderness. After a couple of months of "talking therapy," Dr. Wolff, the tall, gaunt psychiatrist, told me, "You are not responsible for your problems. You have a chemical imbalance. We will treat you with antidepressant pills, and we will keep trying different ones until one works."

Everybody today is conversant with "chemical imbalances" and various brand names of antidepressants, but I had never heard of any of these things. Secretly, I didn't even really believe the doctor. How could my "chemical imbalance" just *happen* to coincide with the horrendous things I'd experienced on LSD? But again, I went along because there was nothing to lose. The period of "experiment" with pills bought still more months of semi-pleasant limbo.

One day one of the pills worked. It was quite sudden. Instead of being afraid to leave the house without my parents, unable to think of anything to say to anyone, I was *filled* with energy and confidence. I marched into Dr. Wolff's office and proclaimed, "Out of the ashes we rise triumphant!"

With all the energy from the pills pumping into my system, I seemed to soon exhaust the possibilities of my home city, even though it was holiday season and many friends were home from college. I decided to go visit old friends from my first school, Northwestern University, in Evanston, Illinois near Chicago. There I had gone through a phase as a political radical (some of this period is covered in the story, "The Incident"), but the end of a love affair had wounded me so that I did not want to go back for my junior year and had transferred to New College.

5.

With my new energy, which seemed to keep streaming no matter what happened, I enjoyed the 300-mile drive from St. Louis. On the street near campus, I ran into a girl I'd known. She invited me to stay in the apartment she shared with a friend and also mentioned, "Aldo (a fictional name used in the story "The Incident") is back in town!" "Aldo" was the radical leader at whose Student Power election rally I had climbed onto a large boulder on campus and told my story of being roughed up by security. He had been elected student president and a few months later had received a letter from the university, saying, "You are disqualified from taking office because of a summer school course you didn't complete two years ago." Disillusioned, he had left Evanston. Six weeks later my roommate and I had received a postcard written on a beach in Mexico. It said only, "Truth is metaphysical, not political."

The next thing I'd heard about Aldo was that he had somehow become connected with Meher Baba, the spiritual figure whose name I'd heard several more times since that day at New College and one of whose books I had even perused, to little avail. After informing me that Aldo was back, my female friend added, "But you don't want to have anything to do with him. He works in an advertising agency now, and I saw him on TV selling laundry detergent!"

That telegraphic description, coupled with the image I'd had of him from before, created a picture that did indeed encourage me to give the fellow a wide berth. How had he possibly changed so much in two years?

In the next two weeks, I visited all my friends in Evanston except for Aldo. Practically every place I went, my host or hostess would point out in the bookcase a book Aldo had brought by, about Meher Baba. Then, instead of discussing Meher Baba, we would continue to go on about Aldo and his eccentricity.

One morning, shortly before I intended to leave Chicago, the phone rang and one of the young ladies said it was for me. The receiver to my ear, I heard a voice say, "Hi, this is Aldo! I heard you were in town, and I'm really happy to hear you're doing well!" I felt immediately disarmed by his genuine and friendly tone. There was no eccentricity about it, only simple humanity. He went on to ask if I wanted to stop by the advertising agency where he worked, to say hello, and I did not feel in the least bit anxious, replying that I'd love to.

6.

The next morning I took the El train downtown to the Prudential Building, where my friend worked. I caught the elevator to his ad agency on the upper floors. Notified by the receptionist, Aldo came out to the reception area and embraced me. Then he led me down a corridor and opened a doorway into what was the *tiniest* private office I'd ever seen.

There were a desk and two chairs in the office—no room for *anything* else. One of the chairs was behind the desk, the other in front. I sat, of course, in the latter. As I faced my friend, I noticed that behind him on the wall was a large poster on yellow newsprint paper. A man's face, in a black and white photo, looked out from the poster. The man looked to be in his twenties. He had long straight hair, a feathery moustache, a wisp of beard and the loveliest soft, clear eyes. Under the photo in large capital letters were the words:

I AM
THE ANCIENT ONE

Below those words in smaller letters, the poster read:

**I WAS RAMA, I WAS KRISHNA,
I WAS THIS ONE, I WAS THAT ONE,
AND NOW I AM MEHER BABA.**

Suddenly I realized that sitting in front of me was someone who could tell me more about this unusual man whose obituary had been read to me for no understandable reason on a misty Saturday morning two years before.

"Did Meher Baba really say he was *God*?" I asked.

"He says everyone and every*thing* is God, but there are very few who are fully *conscious* of that Divinity and who therefore are really able to guide others."

"Why shouldn't I follow Christ or Ramakrishna?" The question erupted out of my mouth. It included the names of two spiritual beings I had recently begun reading about—Sri Ramakrishna having been a great Master who had lived near Calcutta in the late 19th century.

"Baba said he's the *Avatar*," replied my friend. "He said he returns to Earth approximately every 700 to 1400 years, whenever people forget what we're all really here for. In recorded history, he said he had come as Zoroaster, Rama, Krishna, Buddha, Jesus and Mohammed."

"He's naming the greatest figures in history," I thought. I was experiencing a curious phenomenon. Questions had been coming to my mind as naturally as though I were following some kind of script. And yet my words were totally spontaneous. Furthermore, each time my friend *answered* a question, or more accurately, told me Meher Baba's answer, I felt lighter. White birds seemed to be flying upward from my head, so to speak, with every round of our conversation.

This process now stopped. My mind and the room were silent. "Maybe this Meher Baba was a really great man," the voice of my thoughts went on, "but if he died two years ago, what's the difference?" As that thought emerged, a very subtle *presentiment,* came with it—something might *happen* now. That was odd. My sense that "nothing can happen through mere conversation" had led, a couple of years back, to my more dangerous, pharmacologically based efforts at transformation.

"Where is he *now*?" I blurted out, looking at Meher Baba's picture and not even realizing I'd been about to speak.

I waited for Aldo to answer. Silence. In a little while, I looked back toward him. He was smiling. What about? He in fact had practically the widest grin I'd ever seen. I had seen him grinning that way once back in our college days, scruffily dressed, high on LSD and gleefully handing a $5 bill to a beggar.

And then, suddenly, I felt it, too, the—Love! This was Love! Not Romantic Love, not Platonic love with a small "l", but *Divine* Love! I'd read of it recently in Thomas Merton, in Ramakrishna and His Disciples, but without much idea what the authors were saying. This was God!

The room overflowed with Divine Love! The force, the Being, was invisible, yet far more real by far than anything I'd ever known. It felt "pink," somehow, although visually I discerned no color. "I am Meher Baba," it seemed to be saying, silently. It was a distinct Personality; and yet also *included* my friend and me, and everything else! Words like "past" and "future," "me" and "you" had no meaning—only this timeless, all-embracing Love had ever existed.

How had I never before felt what was clearly the only essential fact of all existence? How had I failed to notice Meher Baba, who was and had always been, the Being of my own being, the Self of all?

How long my friend and I sat there, embraced by that divine smile, I don't know. But when I left that room, as it says in a poem I penned several years later: "I searched a different search and sang a different tune."

Postscript

I left that room 45 years ago. Not too long after, I quit taking the pills because I did not really feel balanced on them. I had a girl friend at the time, and came to feel the pills made it impossible for me to give her my true self. I took myself off them, thinking "Baba will take care of me now." But I had karma to reckon with, and spent another year and a half in the black hole.

I don't want to romanticize my life since that profound experience of Meher Baba. Such an experience, resulting in conviction about the Master's status, is colloquially known as "coming to Baba."

However, living the life of literal obedience that Baba asks those who love Him has been compared by close disciple Eruch Jessawala, to "walking on fire all the time." I don't feel I've been able to do that, this lifetime.

I would describe myself as a "spiritual amphibian" climbing out of the seas of ignorance. The stories in this book describe several periods of suffering *after* coming to Baba. What is noteworthy, I feel, is to have been able to recover and go on. Baba said, "All suffering is your labor of love to unveil your real Self."

Honesty demands that I record the life I've actually lived. I feel it IS worth recording: the record of a spiritual novice, finding his way during a period just after the Avataric Advent, a Springtide of Creation when things are possible which during so many periods on Earth are not.

I'm still dazzled by some of the things I've experienced this lifetime. A few of them are in this book, but there are more. It may be that my real life as a lover of the God-Man will begin after all the "dazzle" is gone, and my entire life is, like many of His lovers, "hidden in God."

Meanwhile, *everything* short of God-Realization being Illusion, as Baba says, this life and these stories have, hopefully, a certain honest validity. They have been necessary to live through, as well as inspiring and "educational"; and perhaps they will be of some value to others.

Happy Re-Birthday To Me!

January 17, 2013

Thirty-seven years ago today, on January 17, 1976, in my 28th year, I walked into a room at the Downtowner Motel in Oklahoma City, following Dr. Richard Alpert, a.k.a. Ram Dass. I had an appointment with him the morning after he'd given a talk at the Oklahoma City Civic Center.

I had flown in from St. Louis, and had stayed overnight at a downtown hotel after the talk. I believed my life was over—that if I did not have some kind of brain damage, then I was simply damned. Deep traumatic material had come up from my childhood and had caused me to experience a "nervous breakdown" six months earlier. Five years before that, it had caused an earlier severe breakdown when it had come up on LSD trips. I'd believed my life over then, too. I simply stuck around to see what would happen.

What happened was that a psychiatrist my parents made me see kept giving me stronger and stronger antidepressants. One finally "worked," filling me with energy. With that newfound energy, I had travelled to Chicago and there, had had an overwhelmingly powerful spiritual experience involving someone named Meher Baba, who claimed to be the "Avatar" of our age, a role equivalent to that of Jesus, Mohammed or Buddha in earlier times.

I believe Meher Baba *is* the Avatar, and have tried to follow Him for more than four decades. However, several years after my initial "Honeymoon" with Meher Baba, sexually-charged material about which I felt deeply ashamed, and about which I was unable to speak, came to the surface of my consciousness, and my life fell to pieces. Meher Baba was no longer in His physical body, and in addition to my prayers to Him, I considered whether there was a person on Earth who could help me, for nothing seemed to be changing, and I was quite suicidal. I did not feel I could speak to the ladies who ran the Meher Baba Center about this psycho-sexual material.

I ended up, in desperation, going to the spiritual section of a bookstore, and writing to several authors who it seemed "might know something." One of these was Richard Alpert. At the bookstore, I had opened his book, *THE ONLY DANCE THERE IS*, to a page that described his visiting his brother in a mental hospital—his brother who "believed he was Christ," and that he was therefore entitled to steal people's cars, etc.

It appeared to me that Ram Dass had been *kind* to his brother. I wrote him a letter which said little more than, "Dear Ram Dass, Is there such thing as eternal damnation? I feel my soul is ruined." Things seemed that black.

Two or three weeks later, during which interim I'd moved back to my parents' home from Cincinnati where I'd been trying to finish college (I did, I learned later!), I made a fairly weak attempt at suicide with pills. When I woke up, my mother, on the phone with a doctor, said, "There's a letter for you on the radiator."

In the front hallway, I saw on the mantel of the radiator, a small blue envelope with my address handwritten in ink. The return address was NOT the address at which I'd written Ram Dass in New Hampshire, however. It was a number on Riverside Drive in Manhattan, New York City...the street I'd been born on.

Happy Re-Birthday To Me!

Dear Max,

Your soul is not ruined, and there is no damage to your thought or feeling whatever. Psychologically, you may be a mess, but spiritually you are beautiful and are going to God.

In order to go to God, you have to get all the shit inside you opened up. Why not come to NYC and visit with me? It shouldn't take more than a couple of hours, for starters. It you can't come to New York, write me in detail about your scene and we'll work by letter. Just stay totally open and honest and trusting. God loves you and will show you as soon as you begin to love yourself. Blessings surround you. Accept your own beauty.

Ram Dass

It was about a month later that I went to meet Ram Dass in Oklahoma City. After a bit of further correspondence, he wrote me that he would be there, much closer to St. Louis, where I was, on a lecture tour, and I booked a flight and hotel reservation.

Even as my mother and I ate lunch at a Mexican restaurant on the way to the St. Louis airport, I expressed my misgivings to her.

"I don't really know if he's a holy man, or what he is," I said. "Maybe I'm making a mistake."

"Go," Mother encouraged. We'd made the rounds of psychiatrists, and there seemed no hope there, only dire futures to look towards.

I sat at Ram Dass' talk at the Civic Auditorium, and recognized the perennial message of the Soul's Oneness with God and of life as a spiritual journey to a conscious experience of that Oneness. It was precisely the same as Meher Baba's message. I sat there, though, as though a rain of Love was falling all around, but I was involuntarily covered by some sort of dark umbrella and only my intellect was accessible.

I had spent the morning, after breakfast, walking around downtown Oklahoma City, noticing that practically the whole downtown was in the scaffolds of re-building. I also drew no personal connection to the fact that, everywhere I went that day, on taxicab radios and wafting out of the kinds of downtown storefronts that sold cheap electronic equipment, a new cover of Doris Day's "My Secret Love" was playing, with its last lines, "And now my heart's an open door, and my Secret Love's no secret anymore."

Ram Dass lit a candle in front of a photo of his guru and we sat facing each other.

"What do you want out of this lifetime?" he asked, looking straight at me.

I started laughing nervously. In a moment, though, I realized there was no reason for laughter, that the question was reasonable and I could answer it.

"Release from suffering," I told him.

"Do you want to commit suicide?" Ram Dass asked.

"I don't want to," I replied, "but if no one can help me, I may have to."

Then it looked as if Ram Dass didn't know what to say, like he was searching for words.

And then he asked, almost as an afterthought: "What are you thinking?"

Now, my whole problem was that I was ALWAYS thinking about the "stuff" that was *verboten*, at least in my psyche, to verbalize. There were deep taboos of shame and guilt around a traumatic childhood experience and the various fetishes and phobias it had left me with. The result had been that I was really not able to live any kind of normal life.

Happy Re-Birthday To Me!

Even the compensatory personalities I'd build up had been destroyed, the first by LSD, and this time, hopefully, because it *had* to be dealt with, and GOD would show me how!

I hesitated for a moment. Then I blurted out some of my forbidden stuff! I looked at Ram Dass, to see if he was going to kick me out of the room.

"Ahhhh," he said, and repeated the phrase I'd used. "What else?"

I dug deeper into my, so to speak, bag of shit, and came out with some more goodies. I was not playing around, mind you. I felt this was probably my last chance. And I had to level, and basically, "say all the things I couldn't say." I also expressed what I could in the second person, verbally projecting it directly onto the person right in front of me, so as to insure that I wouldn't start going off into abstractions.

Ram Dass responded "Ahhhhhh," to my second confession. And after that, he seemed to brighten as though actually *seeing* something, and his response was "You're BEAUTIFUL! I love you!"

In ten minutes or so, I had nothing left to confess. I looked within, which prior to that moment I'd been too immersed in our interaction to do. And I saw NOTHING BUT LIGHT! I beamed at Ram Dass! He beamed back. We were just two drops of the Sun!

The rest of our time together that morning was spent creating a plan for me to reintegrate myself into the world, on my return to St. Louis. I was to get a job, lose weight, a little bit each week, accept Ram Dass' love, and write to him and phone him regularly. In the spring, I was invited to visit him in Chicago, and later on in the summer, to come to a retreat he was hosting in Newport, Rhode Island.

Ram Dass was really like a father to me during that critical 6-month period. He was amazingly generous with his time...with his love! I continued to take Meher Baba as my spiritual Master. Originally, I thought it sounded "cool" to think of Baba as my Master and Ram Dass as my "guru." When I told Ram Dass that, though, he said, "I'm not anyone's guru."

Throughout our period of work, he supported and encouraged my connection with Meher Baba. I came to see him, and still see him, as a kind of "specialist" to whom Meher Baba—who once, I'm told, had said to some of His close ones, "Richard is Mine"—had sent me, for a specific purpose.*

My "Ram Dass period" was glorious. The extra weight flew off my body. Everything I did, I did for Love. I had many adventures with this Love. I felt completely safe. It was a case of "Because this person is in the world, I know everything's going to be OK."

Eventually, far into that summer, after my two more visits and many phone calls and letters to Ram Dass, he said to me on the phone one day, "Wow, Max, you sound strong!"

"I *feel* strong!" I replied.

"You know, I'm going back to India soon," he continued.

"Yes, I've heard that," I said.

"Are you going to miss me?" he asked.

I thought for a minute. Then I said, "NO!" and burst out laughing!

He joined me in my laughter. This Love that we shared...it wasn't going anywhere!

---

*In 2014 I was finally able to validate that Baba did indeed say, "Richard is Mine," adding "Many people will come to Me through him." The corroboration came via Ira Deitrick, President of Sufism Reoriented, a group devoted to Meher Baba. Eruch Jessawala, Baba's longtime disciple, had spontaneously shared this information with Ira in India in 1972. Allan Y. Cohen, another Sufi who had had a previous connection with Richard Alpert at Harvard, mentioned to me soon after that Eruch had told him the same thing.

Avatar Meher Baba, 1925

About Meher Baba

Meher Baba was born Merwan Sheriar Irani in Pune, India, in 1894. He was a well-adjusted and outstanding boy. As a college student, he began spending time with an ancient holy woman named Babajan, who sat under a tree that he passed while bicycling home from school. One evening, Babajan kissed him on the forehead, and shortly thereafter, Merwan lost normal consciousness. He later said, "She made me realize the Ocean."

It took several years for him to come back down to the world for his spiritual work. In 1925, Meher Baba, as he had become known (the name means "Compassionate Father") stopped speaking, and communicated thereafter via an alphabet board and gestures. Over the next decades he ran a school, served the poor, the mad, and the God-mad, guided thousands of disciples, traveled the world a number of times, and performed what he called Universal Work. He said that this work would result in a New Humanity, in which human consciousness would rise from the level of reason to that of intuition. Baba became known to many as the Avatar of the Age, the most recent Incarnation of the One who had come previously in recorded history as Zoroaster, Ram, Krishna, Buddha, Jesus, and Mohammed.

On January 31, 1969, Meher Baba dropped his human form, "to live forever in the hearts of His lovers." An online search will find many articles and books with further information.

About The Author

Writer, artist, musician, Max Reif lives in California and shares his storytelling, music and love of play with the preschoolers he teaches and the adults he entertains. He's just released *The Wake-Up Man* music CD and continues to share prose and poetry in The Mindful Word, *The Seattle Star*, *GLOW International*, and elsewhere. For more information, visit Max's website at www.realnothings.com.

www.ingramcontent.com/pod-product-compliance
Lightning Source LLC
Chambersburg PA
CBHW070052080526
44586CB00013B/1030